Daphne - Teach Yourself Driving

Daphne - Teach Yourself Driving

by
L Blair

Copyright © 2017 by L Blair
All rights reserved. No part of this book may be reproduced,
scanned, or distributed in any printed or electronic form
without permission.

First Edition: January 2016
Printed in the United Kingdom
ISBN: 978-0-9935284-4-6

Daphne Teach Yourself Driving

Table of Contents

Table of Contents v
Disclaimer vii
Prerequisites x
Preface xii
Controls Lesson 1
   Controls 8
Moving Off and Stopping 20
   Reversing 28
   Turn in the road 31
   Moving off and Stopping (next stage) 34
Manoeuvres 50
   Reverse park (Parallel park) 50
   Bay parking 55
   Driving Into a Bay (Reversing out of a bay) 59
   Left Reverse (reversing around a corner) 63
   Right Reverse (reversing around a corner) 71
Use of Mirrors and Use Of Signals 80
   Use of Mirrors 80
   Use of Signals 83
   Hand Signals 85
Approaching Junctions and Emerging at Junctions 88
   Approaching Junctions to turn left 89
   Approaching junctions to turn right 92
   Emerging at junctions to turn left and right 96
   Emerging to turn left 97
   Emerging to turn right 99

- Crossroads 102
  - Emerging at a Crossroad to turn left 103
  - Emerging at a Crossroad to go ahead 106
  - Emerging at a Crossroad to turn right 107
- Roundabouts 111
  - Practice - Going Left 117
  - Practise - Going Ahead 120
  - Practise - Going Right 121
- Pedestrian Crossing, Anticipation and Planning Ahead 125
- Emergency Stopping 130
- Meeting Traffic and Adequate Clearance 136
  - Meeting Traffic 136
  - Pulling Up On the Right and Reversing 139
  - Reversing then moving off again from The right side of the road 143
  - Adequate Clearance 145
- Dual Carriageways, and Use of Speed 147
  - Use of Speed 154
  - Overtaking 156

Disclaimer

While Daphne - Teach Yourself Driving has taken care in the preparation of the contents of this document, the information, names, images, pictures, logos, icons regarding or relating to Daphne - Teach Yourself Driving products and are provided on an 'as is' basis without any representation or endorsement being made, and without any warranty of any kind, whether express or implied, including but not limited to, any implied warranties of satisfactory quality, fitness for a particular purpose, non-infringement, security, compatibility and accuracy. To the extent permitted by law, all such terms and warranties are hereby excluded. In no event will Daphne - Teach Yourself Driving be liable (whether in contract or tort (including negligence or breach of statutory duty) or otherwise) for any losses sustained and arising out of or in connection with use of this application including, without limitation, loss of profits, loss of data or loss of goodwill (in all these cases whether direct or indirect) nor any indirect, economic, consequential or special loss.

Daphne - Teach Yourself Driving does not warrant that the functions or materials accessible from or contained in this document will be error free, that defects will be corrected.

If any of these terms and conditions (or any terms and conditions relating to a product or service referred to in this document) should be determined to be illegal, invalid or otherwise unenforceable by reason of the laws of any state or country in which such terms and conditions are intended to be effective, then to the extent of such illegality, invalidity or unenforceability, and in relation to such state or country only, such terms or condition shall be deleted and severed from the rest of the relevant terms and conditions and the remaining terms and conditions shall survive, remain in full force and effect and continue to be binding and enforceable.

This document is for general information purposes only. This document is not intended to be relied upon in any dispute, claim, action, proceeding or for legal advice. It is also highly recommended that new drivers take an approved driver education course to learn the rules and laws of the road, and to develop responsible driving habits. Daphne Teach Yourself Driving are not meant to be used as a substitute for normal driving lessons with a qualified driving instructor. The book is a teaching aid and will help enhance the skills and knowledge required for safe and competent driving.

Published by Daphne Teach Yourself Driving LTD

Prerequisites

Before starting these lessons, some important criteria need to be met:

You must be 17 years of age and hold a valid provisional driving licence.

The person accompanying you in the car must be 21 years or over, driven for at least 3 years and hold a full driving licence. In addition, it is a legal requirement that you are insured on the car that you will be using to practise in.

You must also display L plates which are clearly visible from both the front and back of the car.

If you already hold a full licence, then you do not have to display L plates when practising.

It is also advisable to check your eyesight. You must be able to read a motor vehicle number plate from a distance of 20 metres or 66 feet.

Preface

"Daphne Teach Yourself Driving" complements the App of the same name. Teaching you how to drive step by step, with detailed stages, as if you are having driving lessons with a conventional driving instructor.

This book is designed to help both learners and existing drivers. With the contents of this book while taking your lessons you will learn and progress faster and as a driver you can improve on your skills. As a PDI practising driving instructor you will learn how to structure your lesson, change sentences into questions for your briefings.

The best way forward is start with the control lessons, then moving off and stopping chapters. While practising the moving off and stopping lessons keep practising manoeuvres this will strengthen your clutch controls.

Build upon these basics with approaching junctions, emerging at junctions and then crossroads and roundabouts. This suggested order of learning will promote a better learning experience and an understanding of major concepts of driving.

Pedestrian crossings, meeting situations can be learned at any time. When you are confident with crossroads and roundabouts, you will have mastered all the basics. Improve them with practise on single carriageways and dual carriageways.

For more helpful advice, visit our website at **www.daphnedriving.com** and the **Daphne Teach Yourself Driving App**.

Chapter 1

Controls Lesson

Recognise the safety requirements for setting the car up for you to drive safely this includes. Making sure the doors are closed properly before driving; setting the seats and steering wheel; fastening the seatbelt and setting the mirrors correctly.

Key Topics:

·   The Cockpit Drill (DSSSM), Safety Checks (before moving off)

·   Control Instruments (foot controls, hand controls, auxiliaries and visuals)

This is your first lesson. In this lesson you will learn about the safety of getting in and out of your vehicle and how to set yourself up in the right position for safe driving. We call this the cockpit drill and a good way to remember this drill is by using the acronym DSSSM - doors, seat, steering wheel, seatbelt and mirrors.

Doors

Before entering your vehicle, it is always safer to walk around the back of the car so that you can see if there is any oncoming traffic. It is good practice to have another look around before opening the door. Once seated in the vehicle, it is your responsibility as a driver to make sure that all of the doors are closed securely. You can check this by looking into the door mirrors to see that both of the doors are evenly shut with the panel of the vehicle. In most modern vehicles, if you turn the electrics on (which we will talk about later on in the lesson) you will notice that there is an icon on the dashboard, together with an alarm or a light display to alert you that the door is open.

When opening the car door, check your right door mirror and over your right shoulder, which is where your blind spot is, to make sure that there are no cyclists or oncoming vehicles. If you do not make these checks before exiting the car this could result in an accident occurring. Keep hold of the handle and the catch to prevent the door from potentially swinging open.

Seats

You must now adjust your seat so that it is comfortable and in the correct driving position for you. If the seat is not in the right position, you may feel uncomfortable this may result in cramps or neck and back pains. Most modern vehicles have electric buttons to control the movements of the seat, while others have levers which feel like a bar and are located underneath the front seat in between your legs. If you look down onto the floor under the steering wheel, you will notice three pedals. Put the ball of your left foot onto the left pedal and press it all the way down to the floor. When completely pressed, your leg should be slightly bent by the knee. If it is not, then leave one of your hands on the steering wheel and the other on the bar lever at the bottom of your seat. Pull yourself forwards or backwards accordingly until you achieve this slight bend at the knee.

To adjust the back of your seat to an upright position, you should find a knob located on the right hand side of your seat which you can twist forwards or backwards to get into the correct position. The seat can also be adjusted to go higher or lower for better visibility by using the lever found on the front right hand side of the seat. Now you will need to adjust your head restraint to make sure that the top of your head is level with the top of the head restraint, or your eyes are level with the centre of the restraint. To release the head restraint, squeeze the button to allow adjustment. The purpose of the head restraint is to help prevent spinal or neck injuries. If you do not reach the head restraint, then this is all right as the back of the seat will stop your head from going backwards.

Steering wheel

It is important to adjust the steering wheel so that you can see the instrument panel. If you cannot see the speedometer, you may end up breaking the law by exceeding the speed limit. Also, if your hands are positioned incorrectly on the steering wheel, it may prevent you from carrying out the pull and push steering technique, which will be explained in more detail later on in this lesson. To adjust the steering wheel position, pull the lever underneath the steering column into the desired position. This may vary in different cars. To find where your lever is, refer to your vehicle manual. You should find that your steering wheel can be moved up, down, and pulled towards you.

To find the correct steering wheel position, pretend that the wheel is a clock face. Place both your wrists at twelve o'clock on top of the steering wheel and make sure that your arms are straight. Slide your hands and lightly grip the steering wheel at a ten to two or a quarter to three position. Make sure that you can see the instrument panel on the dashboard. Once you are happy with the position, push the lever back so that the steering wheel locks into place.

Seatbelt

It is your responsibility as the driver to make sure that everyone aged 14 and under wears a seatbelt. Also a child restraint should be provided for children who need it. There is more chance of survival when wearing a seatbelt in an accident. When you have fastened your seatbelt, run your thumb along the strap to make sure that there are no twists in it. This will prevent the seatbelt from cutting into your chest. It is also important to hold onto your seatbelt as you release it so that the buckle does not hit your face or break the window.

Mirrors

There are three mirrors in total for you to use. The interior mirror is called the rear view mirror and is made with flat glass. It shows you an accurate image of what is behind you and is used to judge the speed and distance of vehicles from behind. Use your left hand to adjust this mirror try not to touch the glass as this may cause smudges and make it difficult to see properly. You will be able to rotate it up, down, left, and right. Position it so that you can see the whole of the back window, especially on the driver's side which is the off side. When it is adjusted properly, you shouldn't be able to see the roof of the vehicle.

The door mirrors are made with convex glass which makes objects appear further away and allows for a wider field of view. Most vehicles have mirror adjusters in different places. You may need to refer to your vehicle manual to identify where your adjusters are in the car. If you look into your left door mirror, the back of the passenger front door handle should appear in the lower right hand corner of the mirror. You should also be able to see the back door handle and the side of the vehicle. Adjust the right door mirror in the same way with the driver door handle in the bottom left hand corner.

The door mirrors are used for when traffic is filtering on either side of the vehicle, for example cyclists. You should check your mirrors in pairs, when changing directions, before you slow down, every time you see a hazard and before signalling. The routine used is called MSM- mirrors, signal and manoeuvre. There are areas that you will not be able to see in your mirrors and these are called blind spots. The front pillars holding up the roof of the vehicle are an example of this. There are also blind spots over your left and right shoulders.

To find your blind spot, look in your right hand door mirror, now look over your right hand shoulder, and you will notice that there are objects that you see when looking over your shoulder which you cannot see when looking in your mirror such as vehicles in driveways. This is the same for your left blind spot. When you want to move off, make sure you look all around, especially checking the blind spots, your mirrors, and in front of you. Your last check should be in the direction that you are moving off into.

If you do not use your mirrors, you may cause an accident by crashing into something or injuring someone. Make sure your mirrors are setup correctly and clean, otherwise you will not be able to see properly.

CONTROLS

There are five areas of controls which are the foot, hand, auxiliaries, visuals and dual controls.

Accelerator

Below the steering wheel near the floor are three pedals. The one to the far right is known as the accelerator pedal otherwise gas pedal. You will operate this pedal with the ball of your right foot that is just below your toes. This pedal is very sensitive and should be used gently and smoothly with light pressure for eco-friendly driving. It is used to make the vehicle go faster and operated with the right foot only.

Footbrake

The pedal in the centre is known as the brake pedal. To operate this pedal, you need to pivot your right foot from the gas pedal to the brake. Pivoting means to keep the heal of your foot on the floor in line with the centre pedal, then move the ball of your foot from brake pedal to gas pedal.

The brake is used to stop the vehicle and slow it down. It is operated by your right foot only and is used progressively. When the brake pedal is applied, it will have an impact on all four wheels. Also, red lights at the back of the car will illuminate to act as a signal to other following drivers that you are braking.

You must check your mirrors before you brake to judge the distance and speed of the vehicles behind and at the side of you. If you fail to check the mirrors this could result in an accident.

Clutch

The pedal to the left is known as the clutch pedal and you should use the left foot only to operate it. This pedal is used to move the vehicle and change gears. It works by breaking the link between the engine and the wheels.

In order for the vehicle to move, the wheels need to rotate, and for the wheels to rotate they need a push which comes from the engine. The clutch is used to connect and disconnect the engine from the wheels.

To disconnect the engine from the wheels, we push the clutch all the way to floor. Once the engine and the wheels are disconnected, this will allow you to select the relevant gear. As you bring up the clutch slowly in stages, the wheels and the engine start to connect again. This connection makes the car move which is known as the "bite." At this point you should feel the engine noise get quieter, the front bonnet of the vehicle raises and the vehicle starts to vibrate. This is called the biting point which is when the vehicle is ready to move. You must keep the left foot steady for about six seconds or five mph until the car moves independently otherwise it will stall. Also before stopping the car, the clutch must be pressed all the way down to avoid stalling. If you stall the car, a battery icon will appear in the dashboard.

Biting Explanation

The name "Bite" comes from the idea of eating. Imagine your mouth is open and you are going to eat, so you put food in your mouth. When your top teeth and bottom teeth reach the food this would be called biting but then you have to chew for about six seconds before you swallow, if not you will choke. When driving you need to hold the clutch at the biting point and allow the vehicle to move for about six

Daphne Teach Yourself Driving

seconds or 5 mph before you let the clutch go otherwise you will stall. Stalling and choking is the same thing. When stopping, you will need to do a similar process. Just before the vehicle reaches about 5 mph or six seconds before you stop, you will need to push down on the clutch, otherwise you will stall.

Try and use the correct foot for the correct pedals to avoid confusion which could cause an accident. The brake pedal is slightly higher than the gas to prevent your foot slipping from the gas to the footbrake which could make you stop suddenly and a vehicle crashing behind into you.

Hand Control

Handbrake is also referred to as a parking brake. Most vehicles have parking brakes located in different places. Most parking brakes are located in the centre in between the two front seats. The parking brake is used once the vehicle is stationary to stop it from moving or rolling away. It is also used when waiting or to help you with hill starts. The hand brake only secures the rear wheels.

To practise using the hand brake, you need to press the footbrake with your right foot to make sure the vehicle doesn't move, then with your left hand and left thumb, lift the handbrake up about a millimetre high and press the button. Push the hand brake down all the way to its base. To secure the vehicle release the button and bring up the handbrake in stages to the securing level that is required which is about 4-5 clicks. You should not have to use the maximum amount of clicks to secure the vehicle otherwise the hand brake is not working properly.

The handbrake works on a ratchet system. When the handbrake is applied and the electric is on, a red circular exclamation mark is shown on the centre of the instrument panel located on the dashboard. This will show as a P on automatic vehicles.

Gears

The gear lever is the stick located in the centre of the vehicle, in front of the two front seats, with gear numbers on top. There are different gears for different speeds. An easier way to remember what gear represents what speed is to add a zero to the number. So first gear is from zero to ten miles per hour, second gear is ten to twenty, third is from twenty to thirty, fourth is from thirty to forty, fifth is

Daphne Teach Yourself Driving

from forty and above, and reverse is for going backwards.

To change gears, you need to first push the clutch pedal down all the way to the floor with the ball of your left foot. Then check to make sure the gear is in the neutral position. Using the centre of the inside of your hand which is called the palming technique, hold the top of the gear and move it from side to side and it should move freely. When you let it go it should relax in the centre. Make sure you hold the clutch down while practising changing gears or else you will damage the gear box.

Now look at the number on top of the gear and the line that runs from number to number. Think of it as a train line. With the palm of your hand move the gear lever from neutral, which is the centre position, all the way left and then up for first gear. Second is on same line, so keep the tension in the left direction on the lever then down for second gear. Now with the palm of your hand move the lever to the centre (neutral) you should feel it relax by itself, then from the centre straight up for third gear, and fourth gear is on the same line straight down. And finally for fifth gear, palm the gear lever back to neutral, then move it to the right towards you and then up. For the reverse gear, using the palming technique, move the gear back to neutral then move to the right and down. Once you have practised all of the gears changes, place the gear back into neutral and take your left foot off the clutch pedal.

Please note. Reverse could be at different places in different vehicles, check your car manual. Also, you cannot look at your gears when changing them while driving because you will take your eyes of the road and could result in you crashing into something. A good way of remembering your gears is to think of first gear being located in the front left corner of the vehicle, second gear is in the back left corner, third gear is in the centre front, fourth gear is the centre back and fifth gear is in the front right corner. In the demonstration vehicle, the reverse gear is in the back right corner.

Steering Wheel

The steering wheel is used to steer the vehicle in the direction you want it to go. It works like your eyes, to look left or right you move your eyes. Likewise with steering to go left or right you simply steer that way. There is a special way for steering which is called the pull and push technique.

Daphne Teach Yourself Driving

You can practise this technique by holding a CD or a plate. It is best not to use the steering wheel to practise on as this would be called dry steering which is when the tyres are steered but without the vehicle moving. This may damage your tyres and the steering rack.

Hold the CD in your hands at ten to two like a clock face or hold it horizontally at the centre with both hands. Try to keep your hands in the same position while turning the CD continuously but keeping your hands in the same position. The reason for this method is so you get a continuous steer. When steered any other way and you might lose control of your vehicle and crash. To demonstrate this, hold the plate or CD horizontally or ten to two then don't move the CD/plate just move your hand this time. Keep your hands steady in the same position and turn to the left or right, you should notice that your hands go into a lock.

Indicator lever and wind screen wipers

Most vehicles should have indicator and windscreen wiper levers opposite to each other on the steering rack. Indicator levers are used to give information to pedestrians or traffic of what you intend to do. When the electric is on it will show a green arrow for either left or right and this symbol will be displayed on the instrument panel on the dashboard (we call this giving a signal.) If you hold your left hand on the steering wheel at ten o'clock then put any finger out and you should be touching the indicator lever. Press the indicator lever down to indicate left and bring the indicator lever up to the centre to cancel signal and then up again for the right indicator and back down to centre to cancel.

Windscreen Wipers

Windscreen wipers are used to clean the front windscreen and back window for better visibility with a special wash to help clear the windscreen. If you put your right hand on the steering wheel at 2 o'clock then put any finger out and press the lever up, the front windscreen wiper should operate. The lever can be lifted up in stages for different speeds. To operate the back windscreen wiper, bring the lever towards you. There is a button at the tip of the lever to spray the wash.

Ignition Circuit

There are three different sections to the ignition circuit. If you look to the right just below the windscreen wiper lever, there will be a silver circle with three different points. Within that circle there is a hole to put the key in. Make sure the handbrake is on and the vehicle is in neutral. Turn the key to the first point and this will turn on the auxiliaries. The second point will turn on the electrics, where all the light symbols come up on the dashboard. The next point will turn on the engine which will sound like turning on a machine. What causes the engine to start is the fuel and electrics combined together to produce sparks. Some vehicles may have buttons to start up the engine (please refer to your manual).

Auxiliaries

Most instruments in the auxiliary section are basic. Such as the radio, temperature controls lights, and display button switches. Play around with them to see what they can do and refer to your car manual if necessary. You should also have the rpm, which means rev per minute. The rpm works in conjunction with the gas, so as you press the gas it will tell you how much fuel you are using. It is measured in a thousand revs per minute. One, is one thousand revs, two is two thousand; three is three thousand and so on. Only eleven hundred revs (just above the one on the rpm meter) are needed, to move the vehicle. Two to three thousand revs are used when driving around town and four and five thousand rev when driving on motorways. The more revs, the more money from your pocket.

If the rpm meter is too high and in the red zone (six and seven thousand revs) there may be a risk of damaging the engine. Finally, there is a speedometer dial, which works in conjunction with the gas pedal. The more gas that is used then the faster you go. It's measured in mph, which means (miles per hour) and Km/h (kilometres per hour) you should know the speed limit of the road you are driving on, (refer to the high way code or driving essential skills) otherwise you may break the law and end up in prison.

Visuals

Visuals are all the areas in the vehicle that you can see from such as the windows and mirrors.

Dual Controls

The dual controls are only used by the instructor. They are the brake and clutch and are used just to aid you in your lessons.

I hope that you are looking forward to your next lesson which is moving off and stopping the vehicle.

Chapter 2

Moving Off and Stopping

You will be able to move off and stop the car safely. You will be taught to confidently use clutch control which is the foundation of driving.

Key Topics:

- Moving Off and Stopping

- MSM Routine (mirrors, signal, manoeuvre)

- Safe Positioning

- Reverse in Straight Line

- Turning the Car Around

- Introduction to Emerging at Junctions and Approaching Junctions

Daphne Teach Yourself Driving

Before we start this lesson, it is important to remind you to make sure that the cockpit drill has been carried out which you would have learnt in the controls lesson. Remember to use the acronym DSSSM.

In this lesson you will learn how to move and stop the car safely under control. You will also learn about parking lines and driving lines, how to reverse the car and turn the car around.

Please find a long quiet road to practice on so that you can move off and stop several times.

To help remember the routine of moving off, we use an acronym called POM. Prepare, observe and move. Prepare involves getting the car into first gear, finding the bite and setting the gas. Observe means to carry out six observational checks and Move is when you release the handbrake to move off.

First get your car ready by making sure that the handbrake is fully applied and the car is in neutral. This ensures that the car will not move forward and crash into something. Then start the engine which you should have learnt in the Controls Lesson.

Prepare

Now we are going to start preparing the car.

Using the ball of your left foot, which is just below your toes, push the clutch pedal all the way down to the floor.

After the clutch goes down, using the palming technique, select first gear. Then put your left hand on the handbrake and your right hand at the two o'clock position on the steering wheel. Using the ball of your right foot, gently press the accelerator until it reaches 1100 rpm (revolutions per minute) * which is after the 1 located on the rev counter.

Then hold your foot steady. Start to bring up the clutch slowly in stages about the thickness of a pound coin until you feel the car start to vibrate and the front of the car bonnet rises. The engine will sound quieter. Hold your foot steady. If you bring your left foot up too fast or beyond the bite, you may stall. At this stage, the car is ready to move.

Observe

We now need to look around for any hazards. This involves six observational checks, starting with looking over the left shoulder for the blind spot, then the left door mirror, the rear mirror, in front of you, the right door mirror and looking over your right shoulder. If you do not look around properly, someone could get injured and you may collide into something.

If there is anyone around then you must signal by using your indicator to inform them of your intentions.

Move

If it is clear to move off, release the handbrake.

The car should start to move.

Using the pull and push technique, turn a quarter steer to the right. Let the

car move until you reach the driving line which is about a door length from the kerb or about a metre width.

Then steer to the left and as your car becomes straight and parallel to the kerb, steer a quarter back to the right.

When the car is moving for six seconds or around five mph, it will be independent which means that you can slowly take your left foot off the clutch and press the accelerator with the ball of your right foot and start to progress to around 10mph. It is important to keep the clutch at the biting point for six seconds to avoid stalling. If you stall, this could result in a sudden stop and a car may crash into the back of your car.

Then start looking for somewhere safe, legal and convenient to stop for example, not in front of someone's driveway etc. please refer to the Highway Code for more information.

Once you have decided on where to stop, you need to apply the MSM routine. This is mirror, signal and manoeuvre.

Check your rear view mirror for the speed and distance of vehicles behind you and the left door mirror for cyclists or any other road users filtering beside you on the left.

If there are road users present, then it is necessary to make a left signal to inform them of your intentions.

Following the signal, steer a quarter left until you reach your parking line which is about a quarter door length from the kerb or a quarter of a metre. Once you have reached this point, steer to the right so that the car becomes straight and parallel with the kerb.

Then steer a quarter back to the left to straighten the wheel. Take your right foot off the accelerator.

Using the ball of your right foot, start to brake progressively until the car almost comes to a stop travelling around 5 mph.

Press all the way down on the clutch with the ball of your left foot and take some pressure off the footbrake so that you can stop smoothly. Keeping both feet still, apply the handbrake and place the gear into the neutral position. Cancel any signal made.

Then you can relax and take your feet off the pedals. If you take your feet off the pedals before selecting neutral and applying the handbrake, the car may stall or move.

Parking line

To find your parking line, park a quarter of a door length or a foot away from the left hand side kerb. Open your passenger car door to make sure that you are parked at the correct distance from the kerb. Start to follow the edge of the kerb with your eyes until it disappears from view when it meets your windscreen. This will usually look like it is roughly at the centre of the windscreen.

Driving line

To find your driving line, park about a door length away from the left hand side kerb. Start to look and trace the edge of the kerb again until it disappears and meets the windscreen. This should look around a quarter length of the windscreen from the left or roughly six inches from the centre of the windscreen to the left. If there are parked cars and no visible kerb, then use the outer wheel of the parked cars as your driving line instead of the kerb.

You must keep one metre from the kerb and parked cars in case someone opens the car door. You must keep two metres from pedestrians and cyclists to ensure that you do not hit and injure them.

Once you are around 60 metres from the end of the road, you will need to turn the car around so that you can continue to practice moving off and stopping. The alternative would be to ask your trainer to turn the car around for you. In order to turn the car around, you will need to learn how to reverse.

REVERSING

Before reversing, you will need to make effective observations, looking for any vehicles coming from the front or behind or pedestrians walking around the car. If there is any road user around, you must stop and give them way.

When reversing, you must use a slow speed under 5 mph, using clutch control to maintain this speed. The reason that you must reverse slowly is to keep control of the car and to make sure that you do not injure anyone or crash into anything. When you start reversing you must look over your left shoulder through the back window and also keep an eye in the left door mirror to make sure that you keep a safe distance from the kerb. An acceptable distance will be roughly a foot away from the kerb. You are allowed to take your seat belt off whilst reversing and you are permitted to use one hand at the twelve o'clock position when reversing in a straight line but it is advisable to use two hands to have proper control.

The camber of the road, which is where the road slants on both sides, may cause the car to roll forwards or backwards. If the car starts to roll, press the clutch towards the floor and use the footbrake progressively to control the speed.

When reversing, the same steering is applied as when moving forwards. Therefore, if the car is parked on the left side of the road, and the back of the car is moving towards the kerb, then steer away from the kerb by steering to the right. If the back of the car is moving away from the kerb, then you will need to steer to the left.

Practise

Before practising reversing, make sure that you have parked leaving a distance of five car lengths or fifteen metres behind you. In addition, make sure that your car is parked at the parking line which is about a quarter door length from the kerb. Get the car ready by putting the handbrake on and the gear in neutral. Start the engine.

Using the palming technique, select the reverse gear.

With the ball of your left foot, bring the clutch up slowly to the biting point. Once you feel the bite, release the handbrake and start reversing under clutch control.

Look over your left hand shoulder through the back window and keep checking all the blind spots.

Cover the footbrake with your right foot so that it is ready to be used when you decide to stop.

If the car is going too fast, then press down on the clutch with your left foot about the thickness of a pound coin and if necessary apply some pressure on the footbrake to slow down.

As you reverse try to keep the same distance from the kerb by glancing in the left door mirror. If you need to get closer to the kerb, steer to the left and then back to the right to straighten up.

Reverse back roughly around five car lengths which is approximately fifteen metres.

When you have reversed back for around fifteen metres, stop the car by pressing the footbrake progressively with your right foot and putting the clutch all the way down with your left foot.

Apply the handbrake and select the neutral gear.

Prepare yourself to go forwards and then repeat the reversing exercise again continuously for about 10 goes or half an hour.

Once you have got use to clutch control, you are ready to turn the car around in the road.

TURN IN THE ROAD

Before starting the engine, make sure that the handbrake is applied and the gear is in neutral. Start the engine, press the clutch down with ball of your left foot and select first gear by using the palming technique.

Find the biting point.

Before releasing the handbrake, make sure you make effective all round observational checks.

Release the handbrake, start moving at a slow clutch control speed, steering briskly full lock all the way to the right.

Whilst moving slowly towards the kerb, keep making continuous observational checks.

When you reach the other side of the road which is when the kerb seems to disappear under the right door mirror, start to briskly steer to the left.

Make sure that you take the camber into consideration, pressing down on the clutch with the ball of your left foot and using your right foot on the footbrake to slow down.

Ensure that you stop before touching the kerb. Put the handbrake on and select the reverse gear.

Make all round observational checks again, slowly lift the clutch and find the biting point, then release the handbrake.

Start steering the rest of the way to the left whilst looking over your left shoulder through the back window.

Keep reversing slowly with clutch control until the left door mirror looks like it has reached the centre of the road. This will indicate that the back of the car is close to the kerb.

Start steering briskly to the right while looking over your right hand shoulder to see how close you are to the kerb, keeping in mind the camber.

Stop before touching the kerb, select the handbrake and then first gear.

Make all round observational checks, especially to the left where oncoming traffic could be.

Find the biting point and then release the handbrake. Let the car move slowly until it is parallel to the kerb at your parking line. Then brake gently and press the clutch down to the floor.

Put the handbrake up and place the gear into neutral. Relax.

MOVING OFF AND STOPPING (NEXT STAGE)

We are going to start the moving off and stopping again. Get your car ready by making sure that the handbrake is up and the gear is in neutral.

Prepare

Using the ball of your left foot, which is just below your toes, push the clutch pedal all the way down to the floor.

After the clutch goes down, using the palming technique, select first gear.

Then put your left hand on the handbrake and your right hand at the two o'clock position on the steering wheel.

Using the ball of your right foot, gently press the accelerator until it reaches 1100 rpm (rev per minute) which is after the 1 located on the rev counter. Then hold your foot steady.

Start to bring up the clutch slowly in stages about the thickness of a pound coin until you feel the car start to vibrate and the front of the car bonnet rises. The engine will sound quieter. Hold your foot steady. At this stage the car is ready to move.

Observe

We now need to look around for any hazards. This involves six observational checks, starting with looking over the left shoulder for the blind spot, then the left door mirror, the rear mirror, in front of you, the right door mirror and looking over your right shoulder. If there is anyone around then signal to inform them of your intentions.

Move

If it is clear to move off, release the handbrake. The car should start to move. Using the pull and push technique turn a quarter steer to the right. Let the car move until you reach the driving line which is about a door length from the kerb or about a metre width.

Then steer to the left and as your car becomes straight and parallel to the kerb, steer a quarter back to the right.

When the car is moving for six seconds or five mph it is independent so you can slowly take your left foot off the clutch and press the accelerator with your right foot and start to progress to around 10mph.

Then start looking for somewhere safe, legal and convenient to stop. For example, not in front of someone's driveway etc. please refer to the Highway Code for more information.

Once you have decided on where to stop, using the MSM routine, check your rear view mirror for the speed and distance of vehicles behind you and the left door mirror for cyclists or any other road users filtering beside you on the left.

If there are road users present, then it is necessary to make a left signal to inform them of your intentions.

Following the signal, steer a quarter left until you reach your parking line which is about a quarter door length from the kerb or a quarter of a metre. Once you have reached this point, then steer to the right so that the car becomes straight and parallel with the kerb.

Then steer a quarter back to the left to straighten the wheel. Take your right foot off the accelerator.

Using the ball of your right foot, start to brake progressively as the car almost comes to a stop travelling around 5 mph.

Press all the way down on the clutch with the ball of your left foot and take some pressure off the footbrake so that you can stop smoothly. Keeping both feet still, apply the handbrake and place the gear into the neutral position.

Cancel any signal made. Then you can relax and take your feet off the pedals. If you take your feet off the pedals before selecting neutral and applying the handbrake, the car may stall or move.

You should do this exercise for about an hour, involving the reversing and the turn in the road and use around 10 car lengths or 50 metres space. Practise this exercise until you are able to confidently talk yourself through the process with your trainer.

MOVING OFF AND STOPPING - NEXT STAGE

Once you feel confident with the first stage, we can now move onto the next stage of moving off and stopping. Make sure that you use a long quiet road to practise on.

When the car reaches about 10mph, take your right foot away from the accelerator, press the clutch all the way down to the floor with your left foot. Using the palming technique, with the left hand, select second gear, then take your left foot smoothly off the clutch and put your right foot back onto the accelerator.

Now start to find somewhere safe, legal and convenient to pull up on the left hand side of the road.

Once you have stopped, turn the car around and repeat the whole process again, practising going into second gear. Practise this stage for an hour.

It is important that both the clutch and gas pedal are not pressed down at the same time. Once the clutch is down the engine is disengaged and the car cannot accept gas. This would result in the waste of fuel and

Daphne Teach Yourself Driving

a very loud engine noise. Also, if the palming method is not used to change gears, this could result in an incorrect selection of gear and the engine stalling. It is important not to look down when changing gears. Your eyes should remain focused on the road.

When you are confident with changing into second gear, you can then practise the next stage which involves changing into third gear. If you are not confident changing into second gear, it is advisable to practise some more to reach a competent level.

The next stage involves going into third gear.

When you reach 10 mph, take your right foot off the accelerator, press the clutch all the way down with your left foot, then using the palming method, select second gear. Smoothly lift your left foot off the clutch and the right foot onto the accelerator.

When the car reaches 15mph, take your right foot away from the accelerator, and press the clutch all the way down with the left foot, select third gear and then smoothly lift up your left foot and press your right foot onto the accelerator.

39

Look for a point on where to stop and practise stopping at this point.

Practise the whole process for an hour. This will involve turning the car around and repeating the process of going through all the gears and finding somewhere safe, legal and convenient to stop. Make sure that you practise moving off and stopping for at least six hours.

STOPPING AND TURNING AT JUNCTIONS

We are now going to move onto the next stage which involves introducing you to stopping at junctions, where you are coming from a minor road onto a major road. This lesson will be taught properly when we do the lesson focused specifically on emerging and approaching junctions but for the time being we are still concentrating on moving off and stopping.

The next stage will involve using the MSM routine which you have already learnt.

Using your parking line, park up around ten car lengths from the end of the road. You should be able to see two double white lines and an upside down triangle.

You are now going to move off. Make sure that you prepare the car properly. Ensure that you carry out effective observations and then move your car. Move forward positioning the car to your driving line and at around forty yards (6-8) car lengths), check your interior mirror, left door mirror, signal left, stay at your driving line and start to progressively slow down by using your right foot on the footbrake. Remember

41

to put the clutch down with your left foot before you come to a stop.

By the time that you have reached roughly two car lengths from the double white lines, you should be driving at a speed of under five mph. As the kerb bends to the left, follow it around by steering to the left and keeping one metre away from it.

Then stop at the double white lines by pressing down gently with your right foot onto the footbrake. A good way to judge that you have stopped at the correct position is when the double white lines seem like they have disappeared under the right door mirror.

Select first gear again and find the bite.

Start looking to the right, ahead of you and to the left. Then look all the way back round again looking for pedestrians and other road users especially from the right. If you have to wait for more than eight seconds, secure the car by using the handbrake.

When the road is clear, meaning that you wouldn't cause anyone to stop or swerve around you to avoid an accident, start to move off again, steering to the left into the new road. When the driving line appears

Daphne Teach Yourself Driving

in the windscreen again, start to straighten your wheel by steering to the right and then check your mirrors for the speed and distance of vehicles behind you and cyclists filtering up beside you.

Using the ball of your right foot, press the accelerator and start to progress to ten mph, then take your right foot off the gas, press your left foot all the way down on the clutch and select second gear using the palming technique. Take your left foot off the clutch and put your right foot back onto the gas.

When you reach 15-20mph, take your right foot off the gas, press the clutch down with the ball of your left foot and select third gear. Take your left foot off the clutch and right foot back onto the gas.

We are now going to look for the next left turn which we call approaching a junction from a major road into a minor road. It will help if you start to look for gaps in the road, and for vehicles turning in and out of the road. Once you find your road, at around 40 yards or 6-8 car lengths, start to check your interior rear mirror and left door mirror, then signal left, keeping one metre from the driving line, start to brake to slow down to about 8-10 mph.

Press the clutch down with your left foot, using the palming technique select second gear.

Take your left foot smoothly off the clutch to prevent coasting.

Look ahead for traffic entering the road and look in mirrors again before turning for cyclists. If there are pedestrians already crossing the road, you must give them way as they have priority.

If it is clear to go, when the kerb starts to bend and disappears from the driving line on your windscreen, start to turn your steering wheel to the left. Keep turning your steering wheel until you can see your kerb in the new road re- appear in your windscreen at the driving line. Then start to straighten your steering wheel by steering to the right. Check your mirrors and press the gas to make progress.

Keep repeating this process, going around in left circles, emerging and approaching junctions for about an hour or until you feel confident with the whole process.

TURNING RIGHT AT JUNCTIONS

The next stage involves turning right at junctions.

Once again, park up around ten car lengths from the T junction. Prepare your car, carry out all observational checks and then move to your driving line.

Check your interior mirror and right door mirror. Signal right and then position alongside the centre line. The line should be running below the right mirror or disappearing in the right hand corner of the front windscreen. We position the car like this, so that traffic can pass us on the left.

Using the ball of your right foot on the footbrake, start to brake progressively. When you are around two car lengths from the double white give way lines, press the clutch all the way down with your left foot. You should be doing around five mph.

Stop at the line which should look like it is under your door mirror. If you are waiting, use the handbrake to secure the car. Using the palming technique, select first gear and find the bite.

Look right, ahead and left and all the way back around again. Remember, you cannot cause a vehicle to stop or slow down or swerve to avoid hitting you.

A safe rule to help with your judgment would be to say to yourself that if you can cross the road safely, then you can drive across it too.

If it is clear, move off, making sure that your right mirror reaches the centre of the road before turning otherwise you will be cutting the corner and may go onto the wrong side of the road causing an accident.

When the driving line on the left appears in the windscreen again, start to straighten up the wheel by steering to the left.

Then check your mirrors to judge the speed and distance of vehicles behind you and cyclists filtering on your left.

Start to progress to ten mph, then take your right foot off the gas, press your left foot all the way down on the clutch and select second gear.

Then take your left foot off the clutch and put your right foot back onto the gas.

When you reach 15-20mph, take your right foot off the gas, press the clutch down with your left foot and select third gear.

Take your left foot off the clutch and right foot back onto the gas.

We are now going to look for the next right turn which we call approaching a junction from a major road into a minor road. Once again look for gaps in the road and for vehicles turning in or coming out of the road.

Once you have found your road, at around 40 yards or 6-8 car lengths, start to check your interior mirror and right door mirror, then signal right, position alongside the centre white lines. The line should be running below the right mirror or disappearing in the right hand corner of the front windscreen or if there are no white lines, then to the centre of the road. The car needs to be positioned like this so that cars can pass on the left.

Using your right foot, start braking progressively to slow down to about 8-10 mph. Press the clutch down with your left foot, using the palming technique select second gear.

Take your left foot off the clutch and start to look ahead of you for any oncoming traffic or pedestrians crossing the road.

If it is clear start steering to the right. Make sure that you do not cut corners by lining up the right door mirror with the centre white lines of the road that you are entering as you turn into the road.

If it is not clear to go, then stop the car by using your right foot on the footbrake and pressing the clutch down with the left foot.

When stopping, position the car so that the front bonnet is lined up with the centre white lines of the road that you will be entering. If you are waiting for more than eight seconds, apply the handbrake.

If there is no oncoming traffic or pedestrians crossing, then prepare the car to move off and release the handbrake. Steer to the right until you have found your driving line. Then start to straighten up the wheel by steering to the left.

Check your mirrors and start to progress by pressing the gas with your right foot. Keep repeating this process, going around in right circles, emerging and approaching junctions for about an hour or until you feel confident with the whole process.

Chapter 3

Manoeuvres

For further information, including diagrams and videos see Daphne - Teach Yourself Driving app.

This lesson will show you how to control the car at a slow speed and strengthen your moving off and stopping. It will give you the confidence of parking your car safely.

Key Topics:

- Reverse park (bay and parallel park)

- Left reverse (reversing around a corner)

- Right reverse

REVERSE PARK (PARALLEL PARK)

Before you reverse park you should have learnt to reverse in a straight line. If not refer to the moving off and stopping lesson.

There are a few things to remember before attempting to learn this manoeuvre. You must use clutch control to maintain a slow speed when reversing, under five miles an hour. You must make constant observations so that you can see other road users such as pedestrians and vehicles. If they are in your danger zone, meaning that you could cause them to slow down or stop, then make sure you stop from doing your manoeuvre and let them continue first. If they decide to stop, then you can carry on with the manoeuvre. By doing it this way you can prevent an accident from happening.

You must remember the camber of the road where the road slants. This could cause the vehicle to move faster. Be ready to put the clutch down and use your break to slow down. Remember not to dry steer which means steering the wheel when the vehicle is not moving. This will damage the steering rack and tyres. You are allowed to take your seat belt off when reversing so that you can move around to see better as visibility is difficult when reversing.

Practise

A technique that can be used to remember how to steer when reverse parking is called 1-2-1. One steer to the left, two steers to the right and one back to the left again.

One steer is when the steering wheel starts from the straight position then all the way around and back to the straight position again.

By doing this technique it allows you to park in the minimum space behind a vehicle of one and half car lengths. You are allowed up to two car lengths on your test. When you park, you must try to leave enough space to move off again which is about half a car space. A good way to remember this is to make sure that you could see the vehicle's wheels in front of you.

Choose a vehicle that you want to park behind. Make sure that there is at least a space of one and half car lengths behind it. Then pull up alongside and slightly ahead of the parked car at about a distance of half a door length or half a metre beside it. If you have a greater distance of width away from the car, then when you steer to the left the front of your car will swing too far in the road and may cause an accident.

Select reverse gear so that other road users can see your reverse lights and then secure your vehicle.

Find the bite, make effective observations and release your hand brake. If you do not make proper observations, you may not see pedestrians or cars which could result in an accident. As mentioned at the beginning of the lesson, remember to stop and pause when vehicles and pedestrians are in your danger zone meaning that you could cause them to slow down or stop. Effective observations must comprise of the following; looking over your left shoulder, left door mirror, in front of you, your rear-view mirror, right door mirror and over your right shoulder. When you are reversing, most of your observations must be through the back window.

Start moving slowly backwards until the back of your car reaches the back of the parked car. Your back seat will look in line with the back of the next car.

When you can see this through your rear window and the back left passenger window, then turn one steer to the left. When turning the first steer to the left, make sure that your vehicle's back seat is at the back of the parked vehicle. If you have chosen to reverse park around a car that is faced the other way, then make sure that you can see the front bonnet of the car in your left rear passenger window before starting to steer to the left. You must make sure that you have cleared the parked car before turning otherwise if you turn too early you may crash into the back or front of the car.

Remember to carry out continuous observations.

Keep reversing until your car reaches a forty-five-degree angle. A good way to judge this is when your front door handle looks like it is touching the edge of the kerb. Please note that when you are at the 45-degree angle and your front door handle looks like it touches the edge of the kerb, the closer the handle looks like it is with the kerb the nearer your vehicle will be parallel to the kerb when you finish. At this point, turn two steers to the right while observing all around you. Look into your left door mirror. If you are parallel with the kerb, then turn one steer to the left to straighten up the wheels.

Reverse back a few feet to make sure that you leave enough room to move off again. Then secure the car with the hand brake and select neutral.

The same technique is used for parking on the right side of the road. You just have to remember that you will steer one to the right, then two to the left and one back to the right.

BAY PARKING

It is important that before starting this lesson, you have already learnt how to reverse in a straight line. If not refer to the moving off and stopping lesson. There are a few important points to remember. When reversing, you must use a slow speed under five mph which can be maintained using clutch control. Constant observations should be carried out throughout the whole manoeuvre so that you can keep checking for road users such as pedestrians and vehicles. If there are any road users in your danger zone, meaning you could cause them to slow down or stop, make sure you stop your manoeuvre and let them continue. This will prevent any accidents happening. If they decide to stop for you then you can continue with the manoeuvre.

Remember not to dry steer which means steering the wheel when the vehicle is not moving. This could damage the steering rack and tyres. You may take your seat belt off when reversing so that you can move around to see better, because it is harder to see when reversing.

Practise

Choose a car park that is relatively quiet to practise in.

Stop your car at a distance of a metre or a door length from the bay lines. If you are positioned more than one metre from the bay than the front of the car will swing out wide and this could be a potential hazard to oncoming vehicles and road users.

Pick the bay you want to reverse park into. Do not count that bay but count two bays ahead.

Look through your left window from your driving position and align your car so that the last line of bay number two is in line with the middle of your front door. If the car is properly lined up like this, it should ensure that you end up in between your bay lines. If however, the line is nearer to the front of the door, you will end up nearer to the right line or possibly straddled over it. If the line is nearer to the back of the door you will end up closer to the left line.

Once the car is lined up properly, stop and secure the car. Carry out all round effective observations by looking over your left shoulder, left door mirror, in front of you, rear view mirror, right door mirror and

Daphne Teach Yourself Driving

over your right shoulder. If there are any vehicles or pedestrians coming towards you be prepared to stop and give them way. If they wait, then you can carry on with the manoeuvre.

If it is safe and clear, release the hand brake, look over your left shoulder through the back window and immediately steer full lock all the way to the left (full lock means when you cannot steer anymore).

Keep reversing slowly under five miles an hour whilst making constant observations.

Start looking in both your door mirrors to see whether the bays lines come into view. Once the car is parallel to the bay lines, straighten your steering wheel by steering one and a half back to the right.

Reverse until the front of your car is in the bay which you can judge by seeing the bay lines under the mirror.

If you are not parked properly in between the bay lines, then simply move the car forwards until you can see the lines in your door mirrors. Adjust the steering according to which bay line you need to be parallel with. Then reverse back into the bay and check in the door mirrors that you are remaining parallel with the bay lines.

The same technique is used for parking into a bay on the right side. Once the last line of bay number two is in line with the middle of the right door then steer full lock to the right. Remember to carry out all round observations throughout the manoeuvre.

DRIVING INTO A BAY (REVERSING OUT OF A BAY)

Driving into a bay to park your car then reversing out of a bay into oncoming traffic is not the safest option and is more likely to cause an accident, than it is to reverse into a bay and then drive out.

Practice

First find the bay that you want to drive in to on the left and position one metre (about the door length) away from the bay so you have adequate clearance to prevent the back of the car cutting in and causing damage to other vehicles when driving into the bay. If there are vehicles parked on both sides of the empty bay you are going to drive in to, then leave yourself one and half metres (about a door and a half-length) more clearance away from the bay to prevent both the front and back of your car getting damaged with the next vehicles beside you.

Proceed with clutch control speed under 5mph when your left door mirror seems to equalise with the first line of the bay you are driving into start to turn your steering wheel one and a half steers to the left, which would be a full lock on the steering wheel in most cars. Remember continuous observations throughout the manoeuvre.

Then as your car is getting straight within the lines of the bay, you can notice this by looking in your doors' mirrors to see if the back of the car is between the two bay lines. Then turn the steering wheel one and a half back to the straight position and keep moving until all four wheels are in the bay so you do not obstruct others. If you are not sure if the car is between the lines of the bay then reverse in a straight line as far back as necessary until you can see the two lines of the bay that you have reversed from (these two lines should now be visible in front of your vehicle), then go forward again with clutch control speed under 5mph until your car is fully in the bay. Adjust steering as necessary to be straight, then secure the car and then select neutral.

If you want to drive into a bay on the right do the same procedure, but steer to the right instead of the left.

These procedures are for when bays are on your left and right as you drive into a car park, if the bay is straight in front of you use the left hand line of the bay you want to park as your driving line and drive straight in.

Reversing out of a Bay

Before reversing remember continuous observations and if there are any road users around you (i.e. pedestrian, cyclists, children playing in the car park etc) so keep looking around especially behind you for other drivers entering the car park. Please stop and give way to these potential hazards and if they stop for you then carry on the manoeuvre (see reversing lesson).

Practice

Start to reverse at clutch control speed (under 5mph) keep your steering straight until when the front of your car reaches the end of the bay you are parked in. It's about when the door mirror seems as if it is equalising with the end of the bay then start to turn your steering right or left due to the direction you want to go in next and then reverse for about one metre more so you have enough clearance to drive out of the car park again. If you start to turn your steering wheel too early when reversing, the front of your car will swing towards the bays beside you and may cause damage to other vehicles.

LEFT REVERSE (REVERSING AROUND A CORNER)

Reversing around a corner is an alternative manoeuvre to a turn in the road. The purpose of this manoeuvre is to change your direction. Sometimes you may not have enough room to turn the car around and it is easier to use a side road to reverse into instead.

Before you reverse around the corner you should have learnt to reverse in a straight line. If not refer to the moving off and stopping lesson.

There are a few important points to remember. When reversing, you must use a slow speed under five mph which can be maintained using clutch control. Remember to take into consideration the camber of the road which is where the road slants. This may cause the car to roll forwards or backwards and can be controlled by pressing the clutch down and by using the footbrake.

Constant observations should be carried out throughout the whole manoeuvre so that you can keep checking for other road users such as pedestrians and vehicle. If there are any road users in your danger zone, meaning you could cause them to slow down or stop, make sure you stop your manoeuvre and let them continue. This will prevent any accidents happening. If they decide to stop for you then you can continue with the manoeuvre.

Remember not to dry steer which means steering the wheel when the vehicle is not moving. This could damage the steering rack and tyres. You may take your seat belt off when reversing so that you can move around to see better because it is harder to see when reversing.

Practise

There are two types of corners. One that is very sharp and shaped like an L shape. The other is curved and shaped like a C shape. The shape of the corner will affect how you will steer. Generally, L shape corners will require a brisker steer full lock to the left whereas the C shape corners will need gradual steering to the left. On a practical test you would be asked to pull up on the left before the junction that you will reverse into so that you can determine what kind of shape the corner is.

Sharp Corner

We will concentrate first on the L shape corner. The steering technique that can be used is called half one in half one out (the steering involved is initially half a steer to the left and then one whole steer to make up to one and a half steers to the left which is usually full lock and then half and one steer back to the right).

Using the POM routine which you would have learnt in the moving off and stopping lesson; move off from your parked position.

As you pass the centre of the road that you are going to reverse into, give a signal if there are other road users so that they know your intentions.

Stop about two and half car lengths from the junction and instead of the usual parking distance of a quarter of a metre, pull up half a door length or half a metre from the kerb. The extra distance will help prevent you from getting too close to the kerb.

Secure the car and select the reverse gear. Your reverse lights will show and act as a signal to inform road users of your intentions.

Find your bite using clutch control. Carry out all round observations and if it is safe and clear, release the handbrake.

Look over your left shoulder through the back window as you start to reverse. Make sure you continue to make constant observations throughout the manoeuvre.

Look into your left door mirror and when your passenger front door handle reaches where the kerb starts to bend, steer half a steer to the left.

Daphne Teach Yourself Driving

When the kerb disappears from view in your left door mirror, steer another one whole steer to the left.

Carry out effective observations, particularly over your right shoulder where oncoming traffic could be. This is important because the front of the car swings out when you reverse around the bend which could be hazardous to oncoming vehicles and road users and could cause an accident. Also look in your door mirrors, in front of you and over your left shoulder through the back window into the road you are reversing in. Remember to be prepared to stop and give way for any vehicles and pedestrians. If they choose to wait for you, then you can carry on with your manoeuvre.

When the kerb appears in the back window, start to look into your left door mirror. As the car becomes parallel to the kerb, straighten your steering wheel by steering half a steer and then one whole steer back to the right. Remember to keep the car moving slowly whilst steering to ensure no dry steering which could damage the tyres and steering rack.

Start reversing the car back around two and a half car lengths to clear the junction. As you reverse, try to keep parallel with the kerb by adjusting your steering wheel. If the back of the car is going towards the kerb, then steer a quarter to the right and back to the left again when the car is parallel to the kerb. If the back of the car is going away from the kerb; then steer a quarter to the left and back to the right when the car is parallel to the kerb.

Wide Corner

The C shape corner is much the same as the L shape apart from the steering technique which can be referred to as (one in and one out).

Using the POM routine which you would have learnt in the moving off and stopping lesson; move off from your parked position.

As you pass the centre of the road that you are going to reverse into, give a signal if there are other road users so that they know your intentions.

Stop about two and half car lengths from the junction and instead of the usual parking distance of a quarter of a metre, pull up half a door length or half a metre from the kerb. The extra distance will help prevent you from getting too close to the kerb and hitting it.

Secure the car and select the reverse gear. Your reverse lights will show and act as a signal to inform road users of your intentions.

Find your bite using clutch control. Carry out all round observations and if it is safe and clear, release the handbrake.

Look over your left shoulder through the back window as you start to reverse. Make sure you continue to make constant observations throughout the manoeuvre. Look into your left door mirror and when your passenger front door handle and the kerb make a V shape, steer one whole steer to the left (one steer is when you steer one revolution from the straight position back to the straight position).

Make sure that you can see the bend in your left door mirror whilst you are reversing around it. If you cannot see the bend in the door mirror this will mean that you are drifting too far away from the kerb. Remember to carry out constant observations throughout and be prepared to stop for any road users coming towards you.

When you look in your left door mirror you will notice that the back of the car will start to get closer to the kerb. When it reaches about a foot or quarter door length from the kerb, steer one whole steer back to the right to the straighten position.

Keep reversing slowly until the back of the car reaches about a metre away from the kerb and then turn one whole steer to the left. Make sure you carry out continuous observations throughout the manoeuvre.

Keep repeating this process of steering one steer to the left when the back of the car is going too wide from the kerb and then steering one steer to the right when the back of the car goes too close to the kerb.

When you can see the kerb appear in the back window, start to look in the left door mirror. As the car becomes parallel to the kerb, steer back to the right to straighten up.

Reverse back two and a half car lengths to clear the junction.

When you have finished the manoeuvre, remember to secure the car and put the gear into neutral. Then you can relax.

RIGHT REVERSE (REVERSING AROUND A CORNER)

Reversing around a corner is an alternative manoeuvre to a turn in the road. The purpose of this manoeuvre is to change your direction. Sometimes you may not have enough room to turn the car around and it is easier to use a side road to reverse into instead. Before you reverse around the corner you should have learnt to reverse in a straight line. If not refer to the moving off and stopping lesson.

There are a few important points to remember. When reversing, you must use a slow speed under five mph which can be maintained using clutch control. Remember to take into consideration the camber of the road which is where the road slants. This may cause the car to roll forwards or backwards and can be controlled by pressing the clutch down and by using the footbrake.

Constant observations should be carried out throughout the whole manoeuvre so that you can keep checking for other road users such as pedestrians and vehicle. If there are any road users in your danger zone, meaning you could cause them to slow down or stop, make sure you stop your manoeuvre and let them continue. This will prevent any accidents happening. If they decide to stop for you then you can continue with the manoeuvre.

Remember not to dry steer which means steering the wheel when the vehicle is not moving. This could damage the steering rack and tyres. You may take your seat belt off when reversing so that you can move around to see better, because it is harder to see when reversing.

Practise

There are two types of corners. One that is very sharp and shaped like an L shape. The other is curved and shaped like a C shape. The shape of the corner will affect how you will steer. Generally, L shape corners will require a brisker steer full lock to the left whereas the C shape corners will need gradual steering to the left.

On a practical test you would be asked to pull up on the left before the junction that you will reverse into so that you can determine what kind of shape the corner is

Sharp Corner

We will concentrate first on the L shape corner. The steering technique that can be used is called half one in half one out. (The steering involved is initially half a steer to the right and then one whole steer to make up to one and a half steers to the right which is usually full lock in most cars and then half and one steer back to the left.

Using the POM routine, which you would have learnt in the moving off and stopping lesson, move off from your parked position.

As you pass the centre of the road that you are going to reverse into, give a right signal if there are other road users so that they know your intentions.

Stop about two and half car lengths from the junction and instead of the usual parking distance of a quarter of a metre, pull up half a door length or half a metre from the kerb. The extra distance will help prevent you from getting too close to the kerb.

Secure the car and select the reverse gear. Your reverse lights will show and act as a signal to inform road users of your intentions.

Find your bite using clutch control. Carry out all round observations and if it is safe and clear, release the handbrake.

Look over your left shoulder through the back window as you start to reverse. Make sure you continue to make constant observations throughout the manoeuvre.

Look into your right door mirror and when your front right door handle reaches where the kerb starts to bend, steer half a steer to the right.

When the kerb disappears from view in your right door mirror, steer another one whole steer to the right.

Carry out effective observations particularly over your left shoulder, where oncoming traffic could be. This is important because the front of the car swings out when you reverse around the bend which could be hazardous to oncoming vehicles and road users and could cause an accident. Also look in your door mirrors, in front of you and over your left shoulder through the back window into the road you are reversing in. Remember to be prepared to stop and give way for any vehicles and pedestrians. If they

Daphne Teach Yourself Driving

choose to wait for you, then you can carry on with your manoeuvre.

When the kerb appears in the back window, start to look into your right door mirror. As the car becomes parallel to the kerb, straighten your steering wheel by steering half a steer and then one whole steer back to the left. Remember to keep the car moving slowly whilst steering to ensure no dry steering which could damage the tyres and steering rack.

Start reversing the car back around eight to nine car lengths to clear the junction. As you reverse, try to keep parallel with the kerb by adjusting your steering wheel. If the back of the car is going towards the kerb; then steer a quarter steer to the left and back to the right again, when the car is parallel to the kerb. If the back of the car is going away from the kerb, then steer a quarter steer to the right and back to the left when the car is parallel to the kerb.

Wide Corner

The C shape corner is much the same as the L shape apart from the steering technique which can be referred to as (one in and one out).

Using the POM routine which you would have learnt in the moving off and stopping lesson; move off from your parked position.

As you pass the centre of the road that you are going to reverse into, give a right signal if there are other road users so that they know your intentions.

Stop about two and half car lengths from the junction and instead of the usual parking distance of a quarter of a metre, pull up half a door length or half a metre from the kerb. The extra distance will help prevent you from getting too close to the kerb and hitting it.

Secure the car and select the reverse gear. Your reverse lights will show and act as a signal to inform road users of your intentions.

Find your bite using clutch control. Carry out all round observations and if it is safe and clear, release the handbrake.

Look over your left shoulder through the back window as you start to reverse. Make sure you continue to make constant observations throughout the manoeuvre. Look into your right door mirror and when your right front door handle and the kerb make a V shape, steer one whole steer to the right (one steer is when you steer one revolution from the straight position back to the straight position).

Make sure that you can see the bend in your right door mirror whilst you are reversing around it. If you cannot see the bend in the door mirror this will mean that you are drifting too far away from the kerb. Remember to carry out constant observations throughout and be prepared to stop for any road users coming towards you.

When you look in your right door mirror you will notice that the back of the car will start to get closer to the kerb. When it reaches about a foot or quarter door length from the kerb, steer one whole steer back to the left to the straighten position.

Keep reversing slowly until the back of the car reaches about a metre away from the kerb and then turn one whole steer to the right. Make sure you carry out continuous observations throughout the manoeuvre.

Keep repeating this process of steering one steer to the right when the back of the car is going too wide from the kerb and then steering one steer to the left when the back of the car goes too close to the kerb.

When you can see the kerb appear in the back window, start to look in the right door mirror. As the car becomes parallel to the kerb, steer back to the left to straighten up.

Reverse back eight to nine car lengths to clear the junction.

When you have finished the manoeuvre, remember to secure the car and put the gear into neutral. Then you can relax.

Tips:

If you are still not sure of the difference between the wide kerb and the sharp kerb; when you start to reverse around the corner as the back of the car reaches where the kerb starts to bend, you will need to look in to your left door mirror and the wide kerb will start to form a shape between the kerb and the back of the car that starts to look like a V-shape, whilst at the same point the sharp kerb will start to disappear from the left door mirror.

It is the same points for kerbs on the right, but check the right mirror instead of the left. Take notice that the "one steering in" and the "one steering out" technique is for the wide kerb and is to be used continuously as much times as possible to finish the manoeuvre to go close to the kerb and to go away from the kerb.

If you still cannot see the difference between kerbs, just think sharp because the wider kerbs is hard not to notice with its continually bending shape. While the sharp kerbs bend for brief a moment. The "half one steering in" and the "half one steering out" should be used for the sharp kerbs. Half plus one steering will make a full lock on the steering wheel in most cars.

Chapter 4

Use of Mirrors and Use Of Signals

This lesson will enable you to know what distance to give signals at, you will be able to understand and read signals and demonstrate them. Additionally, you will learn to use your mirrors effectively to prevent accidents.

Key Topics:

·   How, why and when to use the mirrors.

·   Use of Signals (giving signals, why we use signals and reading signals from others)

USE OF MIRRORS

The mirrors are used as part of the MSM routine. MSM means mirrors, signal and manoeuvre. The routine is carried out regularly throughout driving for different situations, for example moving the car, which you would have learnt in your lesson on moving off and stopping.

In the controls lesson, you would have been told how to set up your mirrors properly and how to use them while doing moving off and stopping.

The interior mirror is made of flat glass and shows a true reflection of what is behind you. The two door mirrors are made of convex glass which make things seem further away than they really are and they give you a wider range of view. To demonstrate this, if you look in the rear view mirror at a vehicle behind you and then look at the same vehicle in the door mirrors, you will notice that the vehicle will appear further away in the door mirrors and nearer in the rear view mirror.

You should check your mirrors in pairs, starting with the interior mirror first to judge the speed and distance of vehicles behind you and then depending on the direction you wish to take, the corresponding door mirror for cyclists and other road users filtering beside you. Therefore, if you are turning left, you would check the interior mirror and then the left door mirror. If you are turning right, you would check the interior mirror and the right door mirror.

When to use your mirrors

You need to check your mirrors before moving off, signalling, changing direction/lanes - turning left, right or overtaking, when slowing down or stopping, opening your car door and when approaching hazards. A hazard could be pedestrians crossing the road, junctions, bends or road works.

It is good practise to check all your mirrors before moving off at traffic lights or in traffic. If you fail to check your mirrors properly, you may not see other road users particularly motorbikes which could result in an accident.

USE OF SIGNALS

We use signals to let other road users know what we intend to do. We can do this by using direction indicators, giving hand signals or by reading the signals made by other road users in their vehicles.

Direction Indicators

In the Controls Lesson you would have learnt about the lever located on the steering rack that is used for signalling. When this is used, a green arrow appears on the dashboard. Before signalling, you must check the interior mirror and either the left or right exterior door mirror, depending on which direction you are going to take.

If you are about to move off and there are no vehicles coming or other road users present, then no signal is necessary. The same applies for stopping. It is important to time your signal properly. For instance, if you are planning to move off and there is traffic coming, you must try and signal when there is a safe gap to go otherwise you might mislead road users into thinking that you intend to pull out on them and this may cause them to slow down or brake harshly.

Similarly, if you turning left or right, make sure that you signal in good time. If you signal too soon, there may be side roads that other road users may think that you are going to turn into causing them to pull out in front of you as a consequence. If you signal too late, this may not give the vehicle behind you enough time to react and they may have to brake harshly or swerve to avoid an accident.

A signal is always required when approaching to turn left or right at junctions or emerging from a junction. This should be carried out at a distance of 6-8 car lengths or about forty metres from the junction so that everybody knows what your intentions are. The exception maybe if there is a road marking or sign on the road telling you that is the only way you can go.

On motorways and dual carriageways, the signal needs to be made earlier at 300 yards which is indicated by a sign showing three line markers. You need to indicate earlier because traffic is moving faster. Always make sure that you cancel your signal after use.

Daphne Teach Yourself Driving

HAND SIGNALS

A hand signal may be necessary if your instruments are not working or to strengthen your signal when it is hard to see by others. Also it can be used for the benefit of traffic officers directing traffic.

It is important to check your surroundings for oncoming traffic or objects before giving an arm signal to prevent injuries.

To inform road users that you are turning right, you would wind down your right door window and from your seated position; direct your right arm through the right window. Your arm must be straight, and your hand positioned with your thumb pointing up to the sky to make it easier to see.

To turn left, from your seated position, put your right arm through the right door window and your hand positioned with your thumb pointing up to sky. Then rotate your hand in a circular motion towards the front of the vehicle.

To inform road users that you are slowing down or stopping, from your seated position, put your right

85

arm straight through the open right door window. Facing the palm of your hand towards the ground, move it up and down.

If there are traffic officers directing traffic and you need to inform them that you are going ahead, lift your left hand up towards the front wind screen with the palm of your hand facing up. To let them know that you are turning left, simply put your left hand straight out towards your left with your thumb up towards the sky. Alternatively, you can place your right hand across your left shoulder. To inform that you wish to turn right, you would put your right arm straight out of the open right door window with your thumb on your hand faced up towards the sky. When giving hand signals, make sure that you only signal long enough for other road users to see. If you leave your arm out of the window for too long, you may get injured.

Different forms of signals on vehicles

We can read signals on vehicles to help make decisions early which can prevent accidents from occurring. There are a few signals to observe such as the brake lights which will show up as red lights on the back of vehicles and tell us that a road user is slowing down or stopping. Direction indicators inform road users which way vehicles are going. Fog lights help us to see the road better when the visibility is poor. Reverse lights show up as white lights on the back of cars and tell us that a vehicle is reversing. The horn can be used to alert people of your presence. Likewise, the head lights can be flashed to alert people of your presence. Hazard lights warn road users that there may be danger ahead.

Please try to anticipate and interpret these types of signals early to avoid accidents from happening.

Chapter 5

Approaching Junctions and Emerging at Junctions

You will be able to familiarise yourself with the gears going through the gear ratios upwards and downwards. You will be able to recognise when to stop at specific lines i.e. give way and stop lines.

Key Topics:

- Approaching junctions to turn left or right

- MSPSL Routine (mirror, signal, position, speed, look)

Junctions are where two or more roads meet. You can identify that you are coming to the end of a road by the presence of road signs. You may see a stop sign and a continuous bold white line or a give way sign and double white broken lines.

When you approach junctions to turn into them, this means you will be coming from a major road into a minor road. As you drive on the major road, a good way to find the minor road on the left is to check for gaps in the houses or to look for cars coming in or out of the road.

APPROACHING JUNCTIONS TO TURN LEFT

This lesson would have been introduced to you while you were learning moving off and stopping. You would have also learnt the MSM routine. This routine is going to be used in this lesson but instead of just mirror, signal and manoeuvre, it will now be broken down into mirror, signal, position, speed and look.

Once you have located your road on the left, at around forty metres or roughly eight car lengths, you will start the MSPSL routine.

Mirrors

First you will need to check your interior mirror to judge the speed and distance of vehicles behind you.

Then you will need to check the left door mirror for cyclists and any road users filtering on the left. If you fail to check these mirrors, you may cause an accident and injure someone.

Signal

Following the mirror checks, you will need to signal left to inform others of your intentions.

Position

Start to position your vehicle at a distance of about one metre from the kerb, which is your normal driving line. If there are cyclists or pedestrians present on the road, you will need to give a clearance of two metres. They need more room because they are unpredictable and may swerve or move around.

Speed

Using your right foot, start braking progressively to about eight to ten mph. Press the clutch down with your left foot and using the palming technique select second gear. Then take your foot off the clutch to prevent coasting. (Coasting is when the engine is disengaged resulting in a lack of control of the vehicle).

Look

Look ahead of you and into the road you are turning into for vehicles and pedestrians. If there are pedestrians crossing the road, then you must stop to give them way. Before turning left into the road make a final check in your left door mirror for traffic filtering on the left to make sure that it is safe and clear to proceed. When the kerb starts to bend and disappears from the driving line on your windscreen, start steering to the left. Keep turning until you can see the kerb in the new road re-appear in your windscreen at the driving line. Then start to straighten your steering wheel by steering to the right. Check your mirror in pairs and make progress by pressing your right foot onto the gas.

APPROACHING JUNCTIONS TO TURN RIGHT

The same MSPSL procedure is also used for turning right.

Once you have located your road on the right, at around forty metres or eight car lengths, start the MSPSL routine.

Mirrors

Check your interior mirror to judge the speed and distance of vehicles behind you. Then check your right door mirror for cyclist, motorbike or any other filtering traffic on the right. It is important to check these mirrors to avoid having an accident and injuring someone.

Signal

Signal right to inform road users of your intentions.

Position

Position your vehicle alongside the centre line of the road. To help you judge your position correctly, you will be able to see the line below your right door mirror. Also, the centre line will disappear in the right hand corner of the windscreen. It is important to position the car like this to inform other road users of your intentions so that traffic can pass on the left. (If there are hatch markings in the centre of the road, you are permitted to use them to position properly).

Speed

Using your right foot, start braking progressively to about eight to ten mph. Press the clutch down with your left foot and using the palming technique select second gear. Then take your foot off the clutch to prevent coasting. (Coasting is when the engine is disengaged resulting in a lack of control of the vehicle).

Look

Look ahead of you and into the road you are turning into for vehicles and pedestrians. If there are pedestrians crossing the road, then you must stop to give them way. Before turning right into the road make a final check in your right door mirror for traffic filtering on the right to make sure that it is safe and clear to proceed.

When the right door mirror is in line with the centre line of the new road, start to turn the steering wheel to the right. If you do not line up properly, you may risk cutting corners which could result in driving on the wrong side of the road and being hazardous to oncoming vehicles.

Keep steering to the right until the kerb in the new road appears at your driving line on your windscreen. Then start to straighten the steering wheel by steering to the left.

Check your mirrors in pairs and make progress by pressing the gas.

If it is not clear to go because of oncoming traffic or pedestrians crossing the new road, stop your vehicle with your wheels straight and your bonnet in line with centre line of the new road. This will prevent you from going into oncoming traffic if someone crashed into the back of your car as you would move forward and not into the wrong side of the road. Select first gear and use the handbrake if you are waiting for more than eight seconds.

If you are crossing the path of other vehicles, then they have got the right of way and you cannot cause them to slow down or stop. A good way to judge that you have enough time to turn is to ask yourself whether you could cross the road safely as a pedestrian. If you think you would cross safely then you can also drive across. When you have decided it is safe, move off again ensuring that as you turn the steering wheel to the right, your right door mirror is in line with the centre white line of the new road. Keep steering to the right until the kerb in the new road appears at your driving line on your windscreen. Then start to straighten the steering wheel by steering to the left.

Check your mirrors in pairs and make progress by pressing the gas.

EMERGING AT JUNCTIONS TO TURN LEFT AND RIGHT

Emerging at junction is when you are coming out of a minor road into a major road. This subject would have been introduced to you while doing the moving off and stopping and approaching junctions' lessons. You would have been taught the MSPSL routine. (Mirrors, signal, position, speed and look.) The same procedure for approaching junctions is used for emerging at junctions.

There are different types of junctions. For example, T junctions, Y junctions, Crossroads, staggered junctions and more.

To make it easier for drivers we put them into two groups called open and closed junctions. An open junction is when you can see oncoming traffic from both sides of the new road from a distance of about forty metres from the give way line. A closed junction is when your view is blocked from that distance by parked vehicles, fences, houses, especially in the new road when parked vehicles block your view from seeing bikes and pedestrians. Some closed junctions carry a stop line instead of a give way line.

EMERGING TO TURN LEFT

Mirrors

From around forty metres or eight car lengths from the give way or stop line, check your interior mirror to judge the speed and distance of vehicles behind and the left door mirror for cyclists and traffic filtering on the left. It is important to check these mirrors to prevent any accidents from happening.

Signal

Signal left to inform road users of your intentions.

Position

Position your vehicle about one metre from the kerb or two metres from cyclists or pedestrians. They will need more clearance because they are unpredictable and may move out.

Speed

Start to brake progressively and as the kerb starts to bend to the left, steer with the kerb, keeping one metre away from it to ensure that you do not hit the kerb. Also it will help you to position better when you turn into the new road. Stop at the give way line. You can tell that you have reached this line as it will disappear under your right door mirror.

Look

Start to look to the right in the new road, then look ahead and to the left and repeat this process checking for oncoming traffic, especially cyclists and pedestrians crossing at the junction. Remember if any pedestrians start crossing then you should stop and give them way. It is important that when you are emerging, you do not cause traffic to slow down or stop. A good way to judge that you have enough time to emerge is to ask yourself whether you would have crossed the road as a pedestrian safely. If so then you can also drive across safely too.

If it is safe to go, move off again and keep turning the steering wheel left till the kerb appears in the driving line. Then straighten up the wheel again and check your interior and right mirror as you make progress.

EMERGING TO TURN RIGHT

Mirrors

From around forty metres or eight car lengths from the give way or stop line, check your interior mirror to judge the speed and distance of vehicles behind and the right door mirror for cyclists and road users. It is important to check these mirrors to prevent any accidents from happening.

Signal

Signal right to inform road users of your intentions.

Position

Position your vehicle alongside the centre line of the road. You can tell you have positioned correctly as the centre line disappears in front of the right hand corner of the windscreen and just below your right mirror. It is important to position like this so that traffic can pass on the left and road users know your intention from early on which can prevent them following you and causing an accident.

Speed

Start to brake progressively and come to a stop at the give way line. You can tell that you have reached this line as it will disappear under your right door mirror.

Look

Start to look to the right in the new road, then look ahead and to the left and repeat this process checking for oncoming traffic, especially cyclists and pedestrians crossing at the junction. When it is clear, move forward until your right door mirror is in line with the centre white lines of the new road. Then start to steer to the right until the driving line starts to reappear in the windscreen. At this point, start to straighten the wheel by steering to the left. Check your mirrors in pairs and make progress.

Remember if it is an open junction and you have checked all is safe and clear in the new road; you could emerge using second gear. If it is a closed junction, then you would use first gear. If there are parked cars in the new road which obscure your view, you must creep slowly forward using clutch control to gain visibility before emerging. If you are emerging from a one way road and you are turning left, you should position to the left at the end of the road. If you are turning right at the end of the road, you should position over to the right of the road.

Chapter 6

Crossroads

Learn all about crossroads and recognising the difference between turning right, using the nearside and offside positions. At roundabouts you will learn how to position the car safely and correctly according to which exit you are going to.

Key Topics:

- Continuation of Emerging at Junctions.

- Learn to Emerge at Complex Junctions

- Navigating at Roundabouts

- Using One Way Systems

A Crossroad is another type of junction similar to T junctions. It is where four junctions meet making a cross shape. This subject has been introduced to you while doing the emerging at junctions' lesson. You would have already learnt about the MSPSL routine while practising approaching and emerging at junctions. It is the same procedure for Crossroads.

EMERGING AT A CROSSROAD TO TURN LEFT

Mirrors

From around forty metres or eight car lengths from the give way or stop line, check your interior mirror to judge the speed and distance of vehicles behind and the left door mirror for cyclists and traffic filtering on the left. It is important to check these mirrors to prevent any accidents from happening.

Signal

Signal left to inform road users of your intentions.

Position

Then position your vehicle about one metre from the kerb or two metres from cyclists or pedestrians. They will need more clearance because they are unpredictable and may move out.

Speed

Start to brake progressively and as the kerb starts to bend to the left, steer with the kerb, keeping one metre away from it to ensure that you do not hit the kerb. Also it will help you to position better when you turn into the new road. Stop at the give way line. You can tell that you have reached this line as it will disappear under your right door mirror.

Look

Start to look to the right in the new road, then look ahead and to the left and repeat this process checking for oncoming traffic, especially cyclists and pedestrians crossing at the junction. Remember if any pedestrians start crossing then you should stop and give them way. It is important that when you are emerging, you do not cause traffic to slow down or stop. A good way to judge that you have enough time to emerge is to ask yourself whether you would have crossed the road as a pedestrian safely. If so then you can also drive across safely too.

If it is safe to go, move off again and keep turning the steering wheel left till the kerb appears in the driving line. Then straighten up the wheel again and check your interior and right mirror as you make progress.

EMERGING AT A CROSSROAD TO GO AHEAD

When going ahead at the Crossroad the same procedure is carried out as going left except no signal is given.

EMERGING AT A CROSSROAD TO TURN RIGHT

Mirrors

From around forty metres or eight car lengths from the give way or stop line, check your interior mirror to judge the speed and distance of vehicles behind and the right door mirror for cyclists and road users. It is important to check these mirrors to prevent any accidents from happening.

Signal

Signal right to inform road users of your intentions.

Position

Position your vehicle alongside the centre line of the road. You can tell you have positioned correctly as the centre line disappears in front of the right hand corner of the windscreen and just below your right mirror. It is important to position like this so that traffic can pass on the left and road users know your intention from early on which can prevent them following you and causing an accident.

Speed

Start to brake progressively and come to a stop at the give way line. You can tell that you have reached this line as it will disappear under your right door mirror.

Look

Start to look to the right in the new road, then look ahead and to the left and repeat this process checking for oncoming traffic, especially cyclists and pedestrians crossing at the junction. When it is clear, move forward until your right door mirror is in line with the centre white lines of the new road. Then start to steer to the right until the driving line starts to reappear in the windscreen. At this point, start to straighten the wheel by steering to the left. Check your mirrors in pairs and make progress.

If you want to turn right and there is a vehicle wanting to emerge from the road opposite to go ahead, and then you must give them way as they have the right of way and you would otherwise be crossing their path. To prevent accidents in these situations, make sure that you try and get eye contact with the driver. Look at the way they have positioned and also for any signals.

If both you and the vehicle opposite want to emerge to turn right at the Crossroad, there are two acceptable ways to position your car which are referred to as nearside to nearside or offside to offside. The nearside of the car is nearest to the kerb at the passenger side while the offside is away from the kerb at the driver's side. Usually either method can be used but sometimes there may be road markings with arrows displayed on the road instructing which method to use. The offside position is a safer choice because you are able to see oncoming traffic clearly whereas it is much harder in the nearside position to see oncoming traffic.

When there are no road markings at the Crossroad, try and look in advance at oncoming traffic and the way they are positioning the wheels to help make your decision on which method to use. To prevent an accident from happening make sure that you approach at a safe speed so that you are able to react promptly and adapt to whatever the driver opposite decides to do.

A good way to remember the different positions are to think of the driver's side as the offside and the passenger side as the nearside.

Some Crossroads have traffic lights. You will already have knowledge of traffic lights from a young age when crossing roads etc.

There are three colours used, which are red, green and amber. Red and amber means to stop and wait at the line. Green means to go if the way is clear. When turning right at a Crossroad, if the traffic lights are green, you can move off and position either nearside to nearside or offside to offside in the centre of the road. Alternatively, if there are road markings with arrows displayed on the road, then you must position according to how they are shown.

If there is a yellow box junction at the Crossroad, you are allowed to enter into it if you are turning right and your exit that you wish to take is clear. Sometimes there will be green filter arrows present at traffic lights. This will mean that you can filter in the direction the arrow is pointing if you are going in that direction, otherwise you must stop and wait behind the line.

Chapter 7

Roundabouts

A roundabout is an Eco traffic system that speeds up the flow of traffic when used properly. On approach to a roundabout you will see a large signboard showing the shape of the roundabout. It is usually a circular shape with roads leading off it. When approaching smaller roundabouts, you will see a smaller blue circular sign with white arrows on it. You must always try to go around the island on the mini roundabout and not cut across it because otherwise you may cause an accident.

You would have been introduced to roundabouts while doing the crossroads lesson. Roundabouts are a continuation from this lesson. The same MSPSL procedure that you learnt from approaching junctions and crossroads will be applied for roundabouts.

You can go three ways at a roundabout which are left, ahead and right.

If you are turning left, you should stay in the left hand lane.

If you are going straight ahead, you should stay in the left hand lane.

If you are going right, you should stay in the right hand lane

If there are three lanes in your direction and you are going ahead, stay in the left hand lane. However, the only time you can use the middle lane is when there is a road marking on the left hand lane showing an arrow pointing to the left or if the left lane is blocked by traffic or objects.

You must not use the left hand lane for going right or the right hand lane for going left. This would result in a major accident and somebody getting hurt.

If there are two lanes for going right, use the first lane to go to the immediate right and the next lane to come back around on yourself (back to the starting point).

Counting Exits

The roads that join the roundabout are split into two sections. One for the traffic leaving the roundabout which we call exits and the other part for traffic entering the roundabout where no entry signs maybe found.

When approaching roundabouts, it is important to look out for the diagram. It will show a circular shape with lines coming off it. The length of the lines can be long and some short. One short line would indicate small roads where traffic can leave and enter.

One long line means major roads where traffic can leave and enter.

Two short lines beside each other means that the section you leave (exit) and the place where you enter the roundabout (no entry) are very far apart from each other.

One long line with one, two or more short line beside each other means that the section you leave (exit) and the places where you enter the roundabout (no entry) are also very far apart from each other.

You could have one section with traffic leaving the roundabout and one, two or more different lines of traffic entering the roundabout.

For further information, including diagrams and videos see Daphne - Teach Yourself Driving app.

Therefore, when counting the exits, the places where we leave the roundabout and the places where we enter should be counted as one section.

Please be careful not to count the same section as two different exits and end up in the oncoming traffic and cause an accident.

You will mostly find these types of lines on the roundabout diagrams on dual carriageways.

Remember when counting exits, the third exit and after is a right turn and you should use the right hand lane.

You will need to give special attention to Lorries, cyclists and horse riders. Lorries could position in the left hand lane but be signalling to turn right. This is because Lorries are very long and will require more space for manoeuvring around the roundabout. Please be prepared to hold back and give them more space to prevent an accident. Cyclists and horse riders could be going wide around the roundabout on the left hand edge which could be dangerous especially for traffic leaving the roundabout so please be vigilant and give them space to prevent an accident.

When approaching a roundabout on a dual carriageway, you must give a signal from early at a distance of three hundred yards which will be shown on a sign with three diagonal lines. This is due to the speed as you may be going faster on a dual carriageway and will therefore need to give other road users more notice to inform them of your intentions so that they have time to react, slow down and position early.

Tips:

Take notice that the third, fourth, fifth, six exit and more is right at the roundabout and you should use the right hand lane to approach it. However sometimes roundabouts can only have three exits and not the normal shape we are used to, like four or more exits. The first exit can be ahead and not left because there is no left exit, so approach in the left hand lane as normal and the second exit could be right and not ahead as you are used to, so approach in the right hand lane.

It is very important to look at the diagram and the shape of the roundabout with the road markings before approaching.

Remember no signal on the approach for going ahead only. Please give right signal for going right on the approach and change the signal to left when leaving the roundabout, whilst remembering mirrors, signal and manoeuvre.

One Way System

You can identify a one-way system by seeing a blue sign with a white arrow showing you the direction to travel.

A one-way system is treated the same way as a roundabout but the difference is that you do not have to signal to join the one-way system. You do however, have to check your mirrors and signal to exit it. If you are going left or ahead, position in the left hand lane. If you are going right, position in the right hand lane.

PRACTICE - GOING LEFT

When approaching a roundabout from about forty metres or eight cars length from the give way line, you will need to commence the MSPSL routine

Mirrors

Check your inside and outside mirrors for the speed and distance of vehicles behind you and left mirror for filtering traffic. If you do not check your mirrors properly, then you will not be aware of the intentions of other road users which could result in an accident.

Signal

Signal left so others know your intentions.

Position

Position in the left hand lane.

Speed

Start braking progressively to around 15 miles per hour and select second gear. This gear is initially used on approach as it may be clear on the roundabout and you might be able to go. Remember to take your foot off the clutch.

Look

Start looking for traffic approaching the roundabout from the right, ahead and left. Also look out for pedestrians who may be crossing near the give way lines. Keep repeating the looking process. Remember to give way to the traffic on your right. If the roundabout is clear, you can proceed.

Check your mirrors in the new road and make progress.

If it is not clear, then you must stop at the give way line and select first gear. A good way to judge the traffic and to work out when you have a safe gap is to look at traffic coming from ahead. Traffic on your right should give way to them and that should consequently leave a space for you to go.

Remember to always see for yourself. Do not go if the vehicle beside you is blocking your view. If they start to move, do not use that vehicle as a shield. They may have taken a risk resulting in an oncoming vehicle crashing into you. Also make sure that you have a clear space in front of you before you merge.

PRACTISE - GOING AHEAD

The same procedure is used as for going left but no signal is required for going ahead. You will need to give a signal when leaving the roundabout.

You must position in the left hand lane. If it is safe to go, then proceed onto the roundabout making sure that you stay wide on the left side edge of the roundabout so that traffic can pass you on the right. This will ensure that you do not cut any vehicles on your right. Failure to stay to the left may result in an accident.

As you reach the centre of the first exit, check left mirrors and then give a left signal to let the traffic know you are leaving the roundabout. As you are about to turn in your exit, make a final left mirrors check for merging traffic. Once you enter the new road, check your mirrors and make progress.

PRACTISE - GOING RIGHT

The same procedure is used as for going left but you must give a right signal on approach and get into the right hand lane from early. When approaching the roundabout, commence the MSPSL from a distance of eight car lengths or forty metres from the give way line.

Mirrors

Check the inside mirrors for the speed and distance of vehicles behind you and the right mirror for filtering traffic. If you do not check you will not see the intentions of other road users which could result in an accident.

Signal

Signal right to inform other road users of your intentions.

Position

Position in the right hand lane.

Speed

Start braking progressively to fifteen miles per hour and select second gear. Remember to take your foot off the clutch.

Look

Start looking for traffic approaching the roundabout from the right, ahead and left. Also look for pedestrians crossing at the give way lines.

Keep repeating the looking process. Remember to give way to the traffic on your right. If the roundabout is clear, you can proceed.

Stay in the right lane near the inside of the roundabout.

Give a left signal to leave. For example, if you are going right third exit, when you reach the centre of exit number two, check your left mirrors and give a left signal.

Then start to move to your left so you can come in the left hand lane.

Then make one more final check in your left mirrors before turning into your exit for merging traffic.

Once you enter your new road, check your mirrors and make progress.

If it is not clear, then stop at the give way line and select first gear. A good way to judge the traffic and to work out when you have a safe gap is to look at traffic coming from ahead. Traffic on your right should give way to them and that should consequently leave a space for you to go.

Remember to always see for yourself. Do not go if the vehicle beside you is blocking your view. If they start to move, do not use that vehicle as a shield. They may have taken a risk resulting in an oncoming vehicle crashing into you.

Also make sure that you have a clear space in front of you before you merge.

Anticipation and planning ahead

When driving it is important to continuously anticipate and plan ahead everything that could happen on the road. There are always hazards to be aware of such as pedestrians, other drivers, traffic lights and weather conditions to name a few. A good driver will assess the situation and plan the necessary actions as early as possible to prevent accidents from happening. This will in return save lives, money and lots of time.

Chapter 8

Pedestrian Crossing, Anticipation and Planning Ahead

Understand the difference between pedestrian crossings controlled by traffic lights or a person. Pedestrian crossings which are uncontrolled. You will be able to identify these crossings upon approach and know how to deal with them safely.

Key Topics:

- Recognising and handling Crossings

- Controlled and Uncontrolled Crossings

- Anticipation & Planning

There are many different types of crossings such as zebra, pelican, puffin, toucan, equestrian and more.

To simplify when driving, we categorise them into two groups called controlled and uncontrolled crossings. Controlled crossings are operated by traffic lights and sometimes people whereas with uncontrolled crossings the pedestrian has to decide when to cross the road.

Uncontrolled crossings

We will focus on uncontrolled first. When approaching uncontrolled crossings, you have to carry out the MSM routine. This will ensure that you are aware of the distance and speed of vehicles behind you and of cyclists filtering beside you so that if you had to brake suddenly you could avoid an accident. You should reduce your speed on approach to crossings by four or five miles an hour to give yourself time to look properly for pedestrians and to prepare to stop.

It is important that you anticipate and plan for pedestrians who do not look at traffic and decide to suddenly cross the road late. Look out for warning signs informing you that a crossing is coming up. Zebra striped lines, flashing beacons and zigzag lines are all signs to indicate that you are approaching a crossing. You are not allowed to park or overtake at

Daphne Teach Yourself Driving

zigzag lines. Parking is prohibited because it would obscure the view of pedestrians crossing the road which may result in an accident.

When you see people waiting at the crossing, you must stop and give them way. If you have to wait, then secure the vehicle by applying the handbrake. You must not wave pedestrians across the road as this is misleading. They may not look properly for oncoming vehicles coming from the opposite direction.

Crossings should never be blocked. Therefore, if there is traffic in front of you, try to plan ahead and work out if there is enough room for you to move up without blocking the crossing.

When there is an island in the middle of the crossing, this must be treated as two separate crossings. If you have given way to a pedestrian and they have reached the island, then you can proceed forward as long as there are no pedestrians approaching the island from the other side of the road. If there is no island, you should wait until the pedestrian has reached the pavement at the end of the crossing before you can move off again. This will ensure that if the pedestrian changes their mind to cross back again, you will prevent any accidents from happening.

Controlled crossings

The same rules apply for controlled crossings but you have to anticipate when the traffic lights will change. If the lights are green and you notice people waiting at the crossing, then you should anticipate that the lights will probably change to red and be prepared to stop. If the traffic lights flash amber, you may proceed as long as it is clear and no one is crossing. If pedestrians are crossing the road, you must give way to them.

If there is a person controlling the crossing such as a traffic officer or school crossing patrol, you must obey them and prepare to stop and give way. It is important that you anticipate when the school patrol person decides to move into the road to stop traffic so that you can plan to stop from early.

Remember to use the MSM routine on approach to prevent accidents.

Informal crossings

Informal crossings are islands in the middle of the road to help people to cross. Although these are not compulsory crossings and you do not have to stop, you must anticipate and be prepared to stop and give way to pedestrians who decide to run across or who may have not checked traffic properly.

Make sure that you carry out the MSM routine on approach to all of these crossings.

Chapter 9

Emergency Stopping

To help you to stop safely in an emergency and resume driving when it is safe. You will be able to deal with different types of skidding and how to prevent them.

Key Topics:

- Emergency Stop

- Types of Skidding

When driving on the roads, it is an important part of driving to continually anticipate and plan ahead what may happen. By doing this, you would be able to see and work out the intentions of other road users and avoid doing an emergency stop. For example, you could analyse the movement of children and pedestrians and if you see them looking over their shoulder, this could mean that they intend to cross the road. Consequently, you could check your mirrors and start to slow down from earlier on so that if they do decide to cross, you would not have to brake hard. However, there will be occasions when you may not see the danger and might have to do an emergency stop which would involve braking very hard. If you press the brakes hard this may result in your vehicle skidding.

Types of Skids

There are three types of skids which are braking, accelerating and steering:

Braking Skid

A braking skid is when you brake hard, making the wheels lock and stop turning but the vehicle still carries on moving forward. To prevent the wheels from locking, you need to take your foot off the brake to allow the wheels to move again. Then you need to brake again and release. This is called cadence braking and the process needs to be repeated quite rapidly. However, if your vehicle is fitted with ABS (anti-lock braking system) you just need to brake and keep braking. Abs will automatically release the wheels and brake them again which will help prevent skidding.

Accelerating skids (wheel spin, burning tyres)

This is when you are giving the vehicle too much gas than what is required to move it. To stop an accelerating skid, take your foot off the accelerator.

Steering skids

If you steer aggressively and suddenly while driving, you could lose control of your vehicle.

If the back of your vehicle is moving to the right, then steer to the right to correct the skid. If the back of the car is moving to the left, then steer to the left and this will help to correct the skid.

Factors that cause a skid

There are three reasons that cause us to skid. The first one is the driver, the second is the vehicle and the third are road conditions.

Driver

The driver could cause a skid because they could be under the influence of drugs or alcohol. They may be tired, stressed, young and over confident or old and slow to respond.

Vehicle

The vehicle could be the reason for causing a skid if the brakes are not working properly, have bad tyres and is not road worthy.

Road Conditions

The road conditions could be a factor if there is ice on the road, oil spillages, loose road surface and if it has been raining then the road could be wet.

Emergency Stop - Practise

We call this a control stop because we are practising it safely under control. When doing an emergency stop you should not check your mirrors beforehand because this will result in you losing precious time for braking which could result in the loss of life. Remember, if you are driving responsibly, you would be checking your mirrors regularly and should already know what is going on around you.

It is crucial that you do not press the clutch and brake down together or the clutch before the brake because the clutch will disengage the engine and thus braking will take longer to stop the vehicle which may result in you not having enough time to save some one's life. You must always brake first and press the clutch down before you stop.

It is important that you try not to stall in an emergency stop to prevent another accident from happening. You need to be able to quickly move off again if the danger in front of you has cleared or in case there is a vehicle coming up from behind you.

Emergency Stop - Test Standard

When you are driving at a speed of about fifteen to twenty-five miles per hour, the driving examiner will check around for traffic behind you and filtering beside you. When it is clear meaning that you would not cause anyone to stop or slow down, then a signal will be given which is usually the examiner's hand placed forward towards the dashboard and them saying stop at the same time. When the instruction is given, you should press the brake progressively hard and as promptly as you can. When the vehicle almost stops, press the clutch down to prevent stalling. Once you have stopped the vehicle, apply the hand brake (parking brake) and select neutral. Make sure your surroundings are safe by carrying out all six observational checks, starting with looking over your left shoulder in your blind spot, the left door mirror, the interior mirror, in front of you, the right door mirror and over your right shoulder. Then relax and wait for the examiner to tell you to move off again. Then before moving off, carry out all six observational checks once again to ensure that it is safe and clear to drive on.

Chapter 10

Meeting Traffic and Adequate Clearance

Developing the skills required to learn when and who to give priority to. You will learn how to avoid collisions with other vehicles and objects.

Key Topics:

- Negotiating a Meeting Situation

- Keeping at Safe Distance

MEETING TRAFFIC

Meeting situations are where traffic meets but are unable to pass because of a lack of space. This could be due to parked cars on either side of a road, a narrow road or simply hazards such as cars parking in high streets. To prevent getting stuck, we need to anticipate and plan well ahead. This will ultimately save time, money and lives.

If there are parked vehicles on the sides of the road, it is important that you look out for doors opening, vehicles moving off and pedestrians walking in between the vehicles to cross the road. Taking into account all the potential hazards and the lack of space, it is advisable to use a speed of around fifteen to twenty miles per hour.

When driving down narrow roads with parked cars, it is good practise to scan the road for gaps in between parked cars. If a vehicle is approaching, you must try to give way by pulling into these gaps. If there are no gaps on your side of the road, then simply slow down and allow the oncoming driver to pull up in a gap on their side of the road.

When giving way, try not to pull in too close to the kerb as this may mislead other following drivers into thinking that you are intending to park. Also try not to position too close to the vehicle in front of you because this will make it harder to pull out again and it will reduce the visibility ahead of you. Just leave enough room for the oncoming vehicle to pass you. Remember to carry out all round observational checks before you move off again, especially your right door mirror and your blind spot over your right shoulder. There may be cyclists, pedestrians crossing the road or an impatient driver behind you wishing to overtake.

There are other types of meeting situations. For example, on country lanes you may find passing places where a part of the road is made bigger to allow a driver to pull in to it thus allowing another driver to pass.

There are roads which have signs with a big arrow and a small arrow, instructing drivers who have got the right of way. The bigger arrow means that you have got the right of way and the smaller arrow means that you have to give way to oncoming drivers. To prevent an accident from occurring, please be cautious and allow for traffic that might have already driven through.

PULLING UP ON THE RIGHT AND REVERSING

Crossing the path of oncoming traffic and pulling up on the right hand side of the road facing oncoming traffic is not the safest option to do; because it is easier to cause an accident than just pulling up on the left, but sometimes we have to do it.

In a driving test you may be asked to cross the path of the oncoming traffic and pull up on the right side of the road then reverse to two car lengths and then drive on again.

Procedure

It is the same procedure as approaching a junction to turn right, but the difference is the stopping beside the kerb on the right, so if you are not sure then refer to the "Approaching" lesson. Use the same routine MSPSL.

Practice

Look ahead for a safe legal and convenient place to pull up on the right side of the road (refer to moving off and stopping lesson).

Mirrors

Then check right mirrors, interior mirror for the speed and distance of vehicles behind you and then the right door mirror for cyclists, motorbikes or any other vehicles trying to overtake you.

Signal

Then give a right signal if it is necessary (refer to "Signal" lesson) if there are other road users around signal your intention.

Position

Position your vehicle alongside the centre line of the road. It should be below your right door mirror or the line will disappear in the right hand corner of the windscreen, if you position this way other drivers should know your intention and it is easier for traffic to pass you on the left (remember if there are hatch markings in the centre of the road, use them to position properly). If there are no centre lines then use your own judgment and think where the centre of the road should be (example measure the road from side to side and think where the centre should be).

Speed

Start to brake and lower your speed (example if you are driving at 30 mph progressively reduce your speed to 15/10 mph) getting ready to cross the traffic.

Look

Look ahead of you for vehicles and pedestrians, then have a final check in the right door mirror for traffic filtering. If it is safe and clear to go, start to proceed and turn (a quarter steer) to the right until the kerb on the right hand side of the road start to appear in the right hand corner of the windscreen by the pillar, then turn the steering back to the left and then straighten your vehicle with the kerb to avoid hitting it and cause damage. Check in the right door mirror to see how straight you are with the kerb and adjust if necessary then stop, apply hand brake (parking brake), select neutral and relax.

Remember if it is not safe to go because of oncoming traffic or pedestrians crossing the road then stop your vehicle by the centre line with your wheel straight, (this will prevent you from going into oncoming traffic if someone crashed into the back of your car).

Once you stop select first gear and secure the car if you have to wait. Remember because you are turning across the oncoming traffic, then they have got the right of way and you must not cause them to slow down or stop. A good way to judge whether you have enough time to cross the path of the oncoming traffic is to ask yourself would you cross the road safely as a pedestrian. If you think you could cross safely then you can now drive across turning a quarter steer to the right until the kerb on the right hand side of the road starts to appear in right hand corner of the windscreen by the pillar. Then turn the steering wheel back to the left and then straighten your vehicle with the kerb and check in the right hand door mirror to see how straight you are with the kerb. Adjust if necessary then stop, secure the car and relax.

REVERSING THEN MOVING OFF AGAIN FROM THE RIGHT SIDE OF THE ROAD

Some time when you park your vehicle, depending on the situation, you may need to reverse before moving off again because there may not be enough clearance in front of you.

Test standard requires you to reverse for two car lengths. Not sure how to reverse? Refer to lesson on "Reversing".

Practice

With clutch control speed under 5mph and continuous observation looking around and behind you, then if it is safe then start moving your car back in a straight line. You can judge the line by looking in the right door mirror as you observe to see how close you are to the kerb then keep a quarter metre space from the kerb (so you don't hit the kerb and damage your tyres). Try and keep the space by turning your steering wheel right if you want to be closer to the kerb and left if you want to go away from the kerb and once the vehicle is straight with the kerb, put the steering wheel back to the straight position. Keep going back for the distance of about two car lengths space and then stop.

Then prepare yourself to move off going forward crossing the path of the oncoming traffic to move back to your normal driving line on the left (see "Moving off and Stopping" lesson). Once the car is ready to move, do your observation six point check, this time start checking from the right blind spot to the left blind spot for pedestrians, cyclists and oncoming traffic from in front of you as well as oncoming traffic from behind you from the left hand side of the road. Then if it is safe to go give a left signal if it is necessary and start to move the car turning a quarter to the left until the kerb on the left hand side of the road starts to appear where your driving line is, which should look about a quarter length of the windscreen from the left. If there are parked cars and no visible kerb then use the outer wheels of the parked cars as your driving line instead of the kerb and that should position you about 1 metre or door length from the kerb. Then turn the steering wheel back to the right to straighten your car. Then check mirrors and make progress (remember see "Moving off and Stopping" lesson on how to move off safely and driving line).

ADEQUATE CLEARANCE

Adequate clearance is the space we should leave around our vehicle while driving or stationary. By leaving space around your vehicle you will in the long run save time, lives and money.

When you park your vehicle behind another car or object, it is important to leave enough space to move off again. A good way of ensuring that you have left enough space is to make sure that you can see the wheels or a bit of the road surface in front of you. If you park too close and a driver behind you also parks very close, then you may find that you are stuck and unable to get out of your parked position.

Likewise, in traffic, it is also advisable to leave a safe gap where you can see a bit of the tarmac and tyres of the vehicle in front of you just in case the driver brakes suddenly.

When driving, you should keep a metre from the kerb and parked cars in case someone steps in to the road or a vehicle door opens. This will ensure that you have enough time to respond and prevent an accident. Cyclists and pedestrians in the road require two metres because they are unpredictable. They may fall or a cyclist may swerve to miss a pot hole.

If you are driving through a width restriction (where the road narrows down to 6" by 6" or 7" by 2") use a slow speed by using clutch control. First gear would be best to prevent accidents. This is part of a road calming measure to slow traffic to save lives.

When driving, it is important to keep a safe distance from the vehicle in front of you. A good way to measure this is to give a metre distance (door length) for every mile you travel. If it is raining, then you need to give two metres distance for every mile and if there are icy conditions, 10 metres distance for every mile.

If you are driving above forty miles an hour, you can use the two second rule. Just make up a sentence that lasts for two seconds. For example, you could say,' my car brakes when I am close to you'. You use the two second rule by picking a point on the road in front of you, like a sign or lamp post. When the vehicle in front of you reaches that point then start saying the sentence and if your vehicle reaches that point before you get to finish your sentence then that will mean you are too close and need to give more distance to prevent an accident.

Chapter 11

Dual Carriageways, and Use of Speed

Supporting joining and leaving dual carriageways (including slip roads). You will be able to read the signs and recognise when to change lanes. Through the use of changing gears in 'blocks' you will be more economical with fuel consumption. Learning when it is necessary, safe and legal to overtake vehicles.

Key Topics:

- Dual Carriageway Driving

- Driving Safely at High Speeds

- Understanding Signs

- Overtaking

A dual carriageway is where the road is divided by a central reservation. This could be some type of barrier such as metal, concrete, grass etc that separates you from oncoming traffic.

Differences between a dual carriageway and a motorway

The signs on a dual carriageway are green and motorway signs are blue. On a dual carriageway you can find pedestrian crossings; traffic lights; cyclists; learner drivers and junctions. However, you will not find them on a motor way.

You can merge both left and right and exit left and right on the dual carriageway whereas, on the motorway you can only merge on the left and exit on the left.

Slip roads

Slip roads are used to join and exit dual carriageways and motorways. The purpose of a slip road is to build up your speed when you are joining, to match the traffic on motorway or dual carriageway. Also when you are leaving the dual carriageway/motorway, the slip road should be used to slow down to match the speed with the flow of traffic.

When you are joining the dual carriageway or motorway, you do not have the right of way. You need to check your mirrors and signal early so that the traffic on the dual carriageway/motorway knows that you are joining. Most traffic will change their speed or move lanes to help you join. However, if there is not a safe gap to join, then you may have to stop at the give way line. When moving off again, you would have to make progress very quickly.

When leaving the dual carriageway/motorway, you should not start slowing down on the dual carriage way / motor way because traffic behind may not realise that you are slowing down which could cause an accident. If the traffic in front of you is slowing down, then you will need to adjust your speed accordingly. You must make sure you use the slip road for slowing down. Not all dual carriageways have slip roads.

You will mostly find that motorways join cities to cities whereas dual carriageways are found within cities. You have to give a signal when leaving and joining both dual carriageways and motorways from a distance of three hundred yards which is highlighted by three diagonal lines called countdown markers. The reason you have to indicate early is because you are travelling at a faster speed and road users need more time to react.

The speed limit for cars on motorways is 70 mph. It is a different speed limit for other vehicles for example Lorries, caravans etc, please refer to your driving materials to check.

On a dual carriageway, when the national speed limit sign is shown, which is a circular white back ground sign with a black diagonal stripe through it, the speed limit for cars is 70 mph. It is a different speed limit for other vehicles such as Lorries, caravans etc. Dual carriageways and motorways can be restricted to a safer speed limit depending on the situation. On motorways you would see this shown on the information stands (gantries). On dual carriageways the council will restrict the speed limit with permanent speed signs. For example, a dual carriageway could have a speed limit as low as 30mph.

Remember to keep the overall stopping distance between vehicles for example the two second rule. If you are too close to the vehicle in front of you and they slow down suddenly, you wouldn't have enough time to stop and this may result in you having an accident at such fast speed. Please refer to the adequate clearance lesson for more details.

Changing lanes

On most dual carriageways/motorways, you will find that there are different colour reflective studs on the lines of the lanes. This is to help with visibility at night time. You will find red studs on the left side of the carriageway. The lanes are divided by white studs. Green studs are found on places where you can enter and exit which are usually slip roads. Amber studs are found alongside the central reservation.

Also when there are road works, you will find fluorescent colour studs in between the lanes.

A good way of remembering the colour studs are as follows:

Red is associated with danger therefore you cannot drive on a sidewalk so you would put red studs at the edge of the road.

White lines for white studs between lanes.

On the central reservation you will find all the lightings so you will put the colour of light which is amber. Therefore, amber studs would be located beside the central reservation.

Green is the colour for go. Therefore, you will find green studs for places where you can enter or leave.

In the overtaking lesson you would have learnt how to change lanes safely. When changing lanes from left to right, you need to give a signal to inform road users what you are doing. Remember not to pull out if it is not safe and clear. You should stay in your lane until a safe gap appears and then signal to change lanes.

If there are three lanes on a dual carriageway or motorway you should always drive in the left hand lane unless you are turning right on a dual carriageway or overtaking, then you should return back to the left lane.

When changing lanes do not steer aggressively as this may cause the vehicle to swerve. You must steer smoothly with small movements because when steering at high speeds the steering wheel is lighter.

You also have single carriageways which are normal roads with nothing preventing you from crashing into oncoming traffic for example no central reservations or barriers.

If you put a national speed limit sign on normal roads this will indicate that the speed limit will be 60mph for cars and different for other vehicles. Please refer to driving materials for more details.

When driving, if there is an emergency vehicle behind you, you must try to pull up at a safe place and the emergency vehicle will do the rest. Do not feel pressured to break the law by breaking the speed limit, running through red lights or driving in bus lanes when within operational times as you will be fined. Do not damage your vehicle by mounting kerbs to get out of the way because you may put other lives in danger and cause damage to your vehicle.

USE OF SPEED

The use of speed in driving plays an important part of how we drive in an eco-friendly way. By anticipating and planning ahead, you can use the right amount of brakes and acceleration needed for any given situation which in return will be better for the environment because this will involve less emissions and fuel consumption. Using intermediate gears is also a good way of saving money, the environment and lives. Intermediate gears mean that you can skip gears to match the speed.

In the controls lesson you would have learnt about the speed range of each gears and how to do the palming technique to change the gears. You would have also learnt how to memorise where the gears are located so that you do not have to look at them while driving and take your eyes off the road which could result in an accident.

Practise – changing up

You can move off in first gear and allow the speed to reach above fifteen miles an hour then go from first to third. You can also build up your speed in second gear from fifteen miles an hour to thirty miles an hour then go from second gear to fourth gear. Likewise, you can build your speed up to forty miles an hour in third gear and change to fifth.

It is very eco-friendly to use second gear instead of first to move off when parked downhill.

Practise – changing down

You can stop in any gear and then select first gear instead of going through the gears. If you are approaching a junction in fourth gear at thirty miles an hour and you want to turn left or right, before you turn you can slow down your speed to about fifteen miles an hour then change from fourth to second gear. When driving around forty miles per hour in fifth gear, if the speed limit changes to thirty miles per hour you can slow your speed to thirty in fifth gear then change from fifth to third gear. If you are travelling above fifty miles an hour in fifth gear and the traffic in front of you slows down to below twenty miles per hour, you can change from fifth to second gear for more eco-friendly driving.

Always remember to drive at a safe speed for the road conditions.

OVERTAKING

Overtaking is when we drive past moving road users to gain more progress. You would have been introduced to overtaking when passing cyclists and other slow moving vehicles.

When we overtake, there are three things to consider. Is it safe, necessary and legal?

Safety

When overtaking, you must not make other vehicles have to slow down, stop or change direction to avoid crashing into you. Do not overtake at junctions as there could be vehicles emerging. Also it is harder to see bikes and pedestrians may be hidden between the traffic so by over taking it will be not safe and can result in death or serious injury.

Necessary

If a vehicle in front of you is travelling at twenty-five miles an hour on a thirty miles an hour road, there is no point overtaking just to gain five miles per hour. It will take you a long time to overtake the vehicle and if you go over thirty miles per hour to overtake you will be breaking the law which could result in you losing your license and incurring a fine.

Legal

You must not break the law by driving over the speed limit to overtake. You should not over take at the zigzag lines located near pedestrian crossings because you may put pedestrian's lives in danger. No overtaking should be carried out when there are solid white lines as these warn you that there are hazards. The only exception would be if a cyclist was travelling under ten miles per hour and then you would be permitted to go around them if it is safe to do so. You cannot overtake at double white line. The exception would be a maintenance vehicle travelling under ten miles an hour. You may pass if it is safe and clear.

You should not overtake on the left. You should always pass on the right. The only time you can overtake on the left is when the right hand lane is blocked for example with traffic or when there is a vehicle signalling to turn right. On a one-way street you can pass on either side. You cannot over take where there are signs saying no overtaking.

Practise

The procedure you have already learnt in previous lessons is MSPSL (Mirrors, Signal, Position, Speed and Look). For overtaking, we are going to change that to MPSLMSM (Mirrors, Position, Speed, Look, Mirrors, Signal and Manoeuvre). Then after you pass the vehicle, check your mirror signal manoeuvre to get back in your lane.

Mirrors

Before you overtake; you must check your interior mirror for the speed and distance of vehicles behind you and the right door mirror to check if there are any vehicles trying to overtake you.

Position

You need to position to the right side of your lane beside the line so that you can get a better view ahead and the driver in the car that you are overtaking can see you in their mirrors and are aware of your intentions to overtake them.

Speed

To make sure that you get up to the right speed quickly, you can drop down a gear and by doing this it will give you faster acceleration. We call this an example of G force (if the vehicle in front of you is going twenty miles an hour on a thirty miles an hour road and you are driving behind in third gear at twenty miles per hour, when it is safe to pass, change the gear down from third to second gear to help accelerate up to thirty miles an hour to get that quick burst of speed).

Look

Before you overtake, make a final look ahead of you to check for oncoming traffic, also check to see that the driver you are overtaking has not sped up to prevent you passing. Then look in your mirrors to make sure no one is trying to overtake you.

If it is safe to overtake, carry out the MSM routine. Check your right mirrors and give a right signal and do the manoeuvre.

Once you pass the vehicle, you have to carry out the MSM routine again to move back into lane. Make sure that you give the vehicle that you are overtaking the overall stopping distance space before you start the manoeuvre. Once you have passed the vehicle, you must not move back to the left too soon because if you had to suddenly brake this would not give the driver enough time to react and stop to prevent an accident.

In good conditions, give a metre space for every mile you are travelling at. Make sure that you can see the vehicle in the inside mirror and the left door mirror before signalling left and manoeuvring back to your lane. Make sure your signal is cancelled once you move back to the left and then check your mirrors and make progress.